SPECIAL PRAISE FOR

Healing a Community

"Melissa Glaser's *Healing a Community* serves as a road map for those who unfortunately need to address the mental, emotional, spiritual, interpersonal, and community aspects of a tragedy."

KEN DRUCK, PhD
Best-Selling Author, *The Real Rules of Life*
Grief Coach to Sandy Hook Families

"Targeting the issue of 'what's next?' after a tragedy, *Healing a Community* is a groundbreaking blueprint for recovery and resiliency after large-scale trauma ... a must read for anyone in municipality, emergency-planning, or incident care."

PAMELA H. PRATT, LCSW
American Red Cross Disaster Relief Volunteer

"Although every tragedy and community is different, any town can learn from and prepare for crisis by utilizing the lessons learned and reported in this book. A sensitive, thoughtful guide, Melissa breaks the healing process into manageable albeit difficult steps, addressing the process, the accomplishments, and the difficulties encountered along the path to resilience."

BARBARA LAVI, PhD
Clinical Psychologist Specializing in Trauma and Child Psychotherapy

"A beautifully honest and direct report of what happens in the therapeutic world when a community experiences a mass tragedy. I had the pleasure of working closely with Melissa in her role as the coordinator of the Newtown Recovery and Resiliency Center and I admired and appreciated her skill at navigating the challenges that came with this role."

DORRIE CAROLAN
Founder and Executive Director
Newtown Parent Connection

"As a member of a team that treated the Sandy Hook community after the shooting, I can say Melissa Glaser's book is well worth reading. FEMA had declared the entire town a victim, which was a first, and *Healing a Community* provides an insider's view of the response at a level yet unseen."

J. BARRY MASCARI, EDD, LPC, LCADC
Author Specializing in Disaster Recovery
Associate Professor and Chair of the Counselor Education Department
Kean University

Healing a Community

MELISSA GLASER, MS, LPC

WITHDRAWN

Healing a Community

Lessons for Recovery after a Large-Scale Trauma

CENTRAL RECOVERY PRESS

Las Vegas

Central Recovery Press (CRP) is committed to publishing exceptional materials addressing addiction treatment, recovery, and behavioral healthcare topics.

For more information, visit www.centralrecoverypress.com.

Publisher: Central Recovery Press
　　　　　3321 N. Buffalo Drive
　　　　　Las Vegas, NV 89129

23 22 21 20 19 18　　1 2 3 4 5

Library of Congress Cataloging-in-Publication Data
Names: Glaser, Melissa, author.
Title: Healing a community : lessons for recovery after a large-scale trauma
　/ Melissa Glaser.
Description: Las Vegas, NV : Central Recovery Press, [2018]
Identifiers: LCCN 2018034128 (print) | LCCN 2018035781 (ebook) | ISBN
　9781942094913 (ebook) | ISBN 9781942094906 (pbk. : alk. paper)
Subjects: LCSH: Community psychology. | Community mental health services.
　Mass shootings—Psychological aspects. | Psychic trauma—Treatment. |
　Community life.
Classification: LCC RA790.55 (ebook) | LCC RA790.55 .G53 2018 (print) | DDC
　362.2/2—dc23
LC record available at https://lccn.loc.gov/2018034128

Author photo by Janet Taub. Used with permission.

Cover and interior design by Marisa Jackson. Cover image © Erika Pochybova.

DEDICATED TO HILDA PLAUT,
MARIANNE COHEN, AND WILL COHEN

TABLE OF CONTENTS

PART II: INDIVIDUALIZING RECOVERY

FOREWORD

I was on a plane headed home on October 1, 2017, when mass tragedy struck my community, Las Vegas, Nevada. A lone gunman killed fifty-eight people and injured 851 more at the Route 91 Harvest festival outside the Mandalay Bay resort. It was, to date, the deadliest mass shooting in modern US history, and the emotional and mental trauma people in the community have suffered in the aftermath is staggering. A book like Melissa Glaser's *Healing a Community* would have helped prepare us for the recovery effort, which is ongoing. Many parallels exist between what happened in Newtown and Las Vegas, as different as the two places are, so I recommend this book to anyone in a position to help their community should tragedy strike.

When I landed at McCarran Airport in Las Vegas, it was immediately clear that no one knew how to handle the confusion, chaos, and anguish people were suffering there. As a psychotherapist trained in crisis intervention, I would help the survivors seek solace and comfort in the days and months to come. Las Vegas had never experienced this type of crisis, or one of such magnitude, so the whole city was in shock, and from the moment the incident occurred, it was apparent there would be a long recovery process with many unknown variables.

Some of the questions were logistical. Who was in charge? Where should we go to provide crisis intervention therapy? Who would be the direct point of contact? As a result, I was sent to multiple locations and initially unable to help due to poor planning. Las Vegas has long been recognized as a potential target for terrorist attacks, yet how a large-scale recovery effort might work was not considered in advance. Therapists committed to see individuals in their private practices and on site, at crisis management locations, but direction was often unclear and funds were not readily available. Without any real coordination, we worked together to make sure all aspects of the victims' needs were being met.

Once a group was established to facilitate support teams, I connected with them and began doing crisis intervention work on a team of therapists at a resiliency center that was born out of the shooting and funded through state, county, and federal grants. The victims would tell me devastating stories about the fear they experienced. A feeling of safety is extremely important for individuals who have witnessed death and destruction and who are in shock. That sense of security was taken that night. And the recovery process continues to this day, more than a year after the shooting.

In *Healing a Community*, Melissa Glaser gives an effective overview of this process. She highlights the importance of identifying professionals in the impacted community who are qualified to provide support, as well as many other important strategies that should be put in place to direct interventions in a time of crisis. This information would have been invaluable to Las Vegas in October of 2017. The topics she covers address many of the issues we faced, namely how best to provide therapeutic support to the public. Having a guideline to follow, such as the one provided in this book, might have helped us to establish a direct line of management for therapeutic services and provide guidance in light of the emotional, political, financial, and social complications we experienced in the weeks and months afterward.

Melissa navigated the aftermath of the Newtown community's shooting with determination, compassion, and an understanding that it wouldn't be the same place it was prior to the Sandy Hook shooting. That place was lost forever. However, she helped inspire the community to come together, support one another, and remain committed to the healing process. These efforts demonstrated what it takes to create a sense of resiliency, and she helped those touched by the tragedy grow after their unimaginable losses.

It is no small feat to run a resiliency center. In this role, Melissa coordinated programs and services that involved sensitive interactions with government officials, the victims and their families, clinical practitioners, businesses, and philanthropic organizations. The politics surrounding the tragic event are conveyed here with honesty, integrity, and grace. The outcome of her work in tackling such a challenging position is this book—a much-needed guide for mental health recovery for communities that have experienced large-scale tragedy.

In a perfect world, we wouldn't need a guidebook on the mental health response to a violent atrocity. But sadly, in our current society, we do need this book. It's a necessary resource for every community that wants to be prepared for horrific occurrences. In fact, it is the only book available today in the mental health community that outlines the exact process to begin the road to recovery after such a calamitous event.

About a year after my city was devastated in the Route 91 massacre, I received a call from someone who said she was finally ready to seek help for the fear and loss she had suffered since that tragic night below the Mandalay Bay. When we met, she revealed multiple concerns. She often heard gunshots in her sleep, was unable to rest, and gradually her quality of life had eroded. Trauma isn't always easy to see, but it profoundly impacts the daily lives of countless people touched by violence and other kinds of traumatic experiences. In this unfortunate context, Melissa's book helps bring to light the importance of ensuring that those who need help after a mass tragedy are not forgotten, whatever their needs may be.

Healing a Community covers the early stages of what should happen to alleviate trauma from a mass tragedy, but also brings awareness to how the therapeutic process needs to occur in the months and years to come to bring about true recovery. It can take that long for some people to go about their days without thinking of the loss they suffered. The trauma impact may manifest as a debilitating fear that plagues their daily lives, and there's no telling when it will stop.

As individuals lose their innocence, so does their community. But that doesn't mean hope and resiliency are permanently lost. Reading this book can assist in the hard work of bringing people together after a mass tragedy with the goal of healthy healing.

AMY REAM, MFT
Las Vegas, Nevada

ACKNOWLEDGMENTS

First and foremost, I wish to express my gratitude to the families and residents of Newtown for allowing me to step into my role as the Recovery and Resiliency Coordinator and learn from their truly gracious example of compassion, empathy, and courage. I was fortunate to meet so many beautiful individuals who instinctively surrounded their community with care and provided a path for me to walk through as I tried to make a difference in the aftermath of this unspeakable tragedy.

The Walnut Hill Community Church stepped forward to provide some initial funding for this project without expectations on the outcome. I would never have been able to take this project on without their support.

I am forever appreciative for the guidance, expertise, competence, and enthusiasm I received from my agent Gareth Esersky and Pam Liflander, who helped me put my thoughts on these pages. They encouraged me to stay steady to this project and believed that this book would make a valuable contribution to many communities in need of guidance and support. They worked behind the scenes to champion it and held me accountable to seeing the bigger picture. This book would not have come to fruition without their efforts.

I would like to thank Central Recovery Press for their serious commitment to this subject and their steady counsel and direction.

I will always be indebted to the work and commitment of my skilled Recovery and Resiliency Team. This team—Deb Del Vecchio-Scully, Catherine Galda, Eileen Rondeau, Suzy DeYoung, and Margot Robins—showed up every day with open hearts for all those in need of healing. Without their professionalism, steadfast caring, and skilled presence, the work would have surely fallen flat. Their support of my role was invaluable when I needed it most.

There were many selfless individuals, clinicians and healers, mentors and community activists, neighbors and teachers who gave of themselves continuously to make a positive impact on the lives of the many people who were affected by this tragedy. Many of these individuals still show up and say yes to requests for assistance. They are the true heroes in this work.

Finally, I wish to acknowledge my husband Matthew and my sons Sam, Jake, and Dan. They were always encouraging and willing to accept less of my attention while I worked on this book between an already impossible schedule. Matt's love and moral support made the time and effort a little more tolerable. Their laughter at the end of a heavy day forced me to keep the balance in my life.

INTRODUCTION

When I began my licensed therapy practice back in 1991, I never imagined that I would someday live in a world where mass shootings occur dozens of times each year. In 2015, *The Washington Post* reported that during President Obama's second term, no single Sunday-to-Saturday calendar week passed without a mass-shooting incident. And since then, the violence has proliferated at airports, schools, and malls, not only in the US but around the world. What's more, natural disasters such as hurricanes, mudslides, and wildfires significantly affect communities well after the initial incident, causing mental health problems for large portions of the impacted populations.

Despite their best intentions, most clinicians are not adequately trained to work with people suffering from complicated grief and complex trauma, the psychological phenomena that often result from these tragedies. Most therapists have not practiced in situations in which hundreds of people are affected at the same time, so why would they have sought such knowledge? Yet in the world we now inhabit, the need to prepare for those circumstances is great. The unfortunate lesson I learned in Newtown, Connecticut following the Sandy Hook School (SHS) shooting is that every community needs to create a mental health recovery plan so that its leaders, therapists, and families know what to do if a large-scale tragedy occurs.

NEWTOWN'S STORY

Newtown was, and is, quintessential New England. It's lined with residential neighborhoods, multiple churches and other houses of worship, boutique shops, restaurants, and picturesque Colonial houses and buildings. There is a huge flagpole in the middle of a roundabout on Main Street. Located in Fairfield County, Connecticut, Newtown stands apart in its quiet charm from what is otherwise known as the Gold Coast of Connecticut. Surrounded by farms and rolling hills, Newtown was founded in 1705 and incorporated in 1711. Today, it's the fifth largest town in Connecticut, covering sixty square miles. For its 28,000 residents, Newtown provides a safe haven to raise a family away from the hustle of New York City, Hartford, and Boston. Violent crime was virtually unheard of in its quaint environs until December 14, 2012, when Newtown changed forever.

That morning, at approximately 9:35a.m., twenty-year-old resident Adam Lanza entered his neighborhood Sandy Hook Elementary School after shooting and killing his mother in their home. Armed with a high-caliber rifle, he shot his way through the locked glass front doors of what was his former grade school. The principal raced into the hallway, the public address system in the front office still turned on for the morning announcements. Lanza immediately shot and killed the principal and a school psychologist, and injured another educational professional, all of whom had run to the school entryway upon hearing the initial gunfire. Heroically, they had tried to stop the shooter before he could harm others. But in less than five minutes, Lanza gained access to two first grade classrooms off the school's main corridor, where he killed twenty students, two teachers, and two teacher's aides in quick succession, firing 156 shots from one rifle and two more from a pistol. Lanza killed himself then, just as emergency responders were arriving to the scene.

The school was evacuated immediately after the shooting. Teachers and staff raced surviving children to a nearby firehouse. As reports of the shooting spread through town, frantic parents descended on the site. By nightfall the firehouse had become a gathering place for the entire community, including parents and family members who had lost loved ones.

This heartbreaking tragedy remains one of the country's most devastating massacres. At the time it occurred, it was the second-deadliest mass shooting in modern US history, a statistic that has since been surpassed. More than six years later, the names Newtown and Sandy Hook continue to spark horrific memories for countless Americans. In a tearful statement delivered on the night of the shooting, President Obama said, "Our hearts are broken today—for the parents and grandparents, sisters and brothers of these little children, and for the families of the adults who were lost. Our hearts are broken for the parents of the survivors as well, for as blessed as they are to have their children home tonight, they know that their children's innocence has been torn away from them too early, and there are no words that will ease their pain."

CHAOS AND DISAGREEMENT IN THE IMMEDIATE AFTERMATH

The Sandy Hook neighborhood, as well as the greater Newtown community, was inextricably altered by the event. The recovery effort began immediately. It still continues today. And one of many important lessons to come out of the process was that even the best-intentioned remedies, when put in place without a clear, long-term plan, can have devastating effects.

The local and national response to the shooting was overwhelming. Without underlying town-wide disaster plans, Newtown officials quickly developed collaborative partnerships to address the Sandy Hook School community and Newtown residents' needs. The town was flooded with donations, money, volunteers, and well-meaning providers. But while some added value, others actually hindered the response. For instance, the Reed Intermediate School was transformed into a mental health triage and crisis intervention center staffed by Newtown Youth & Family Services, clinicians from the Red Cross, behavioral healthcare providers from the immediate community and the rest of the country, and the Department of Mental Health and Addiction Services (DMHAS). This influx of support was appreciated, yet chaotic and ultimately ineffective. There was no organization, and even experts were not always clear on their roles. Communication among the groups was often splintered or fragmented, credentials were not always vetted, and in a short period of time this level of support began to deteriorate.

The tendency is for people to come together quickly after a tragedy to offer their assistance. Yet with no designated liaison or gatekeeper, communication can break down and result in a fractured system rather than a cohesive network. People don't know who is in charge or where to go for help. Questions about trust, overlap, and service duplication surface. This breeds a culture of informal dialogue and assumptions about who is eligible for assistance and which groups have the greatest need. Providers may feel minimized or excluded from the recovery network. Competition and distrust can ensue.

There was also the question of what to do with the building. Sandy Hook closed immediately after the shooting, and the surviving children were temporarily enrolled at a school in a neighboring town. Then, six months later, Newtown voted to have the Sandy Hook School building torn down and replaced with a new one on the same footprint. Yet once construction began, there was tremendous emotional upheaval. The idea of a schoolhouse sitting at the same location became a trigger for Sandy Hook School personnel as well as some parents and students. Residents would drive to the construction site and sit in their cars and cry. Teachers questioned whether they could return to the location. Nearly four years after the massacre, when the project was finished, everything about the new building showed careful planning and tremendous sensitivity. The design also included state-of-the-art security systems. But many teachers and families still had a hard time driving to the site of such a horrific chain of events.

MONEY TO ADDRESS RECOVERY NEEDS

In January 2013, just a month after the shooting, the federal Office of Victim Services and the Department of Justice suggested that Newtown file a proposal to access federal financial aid to support their recovery. A community needs assessment was completed later that year; it stated that the mental and physical health needs for the community would be long term, given the age of the victims and the horror of the circumstances. The community applied for the Department of Justice grant, which would become the first of its kind to address the mental health needs of an entire community. The application included proposals from organizations for continued programming funds.

Eighteen months later, the town government of Newtown received $7 million from the federal government to address "consequence management related to the tragedy." A large portion of the grant went to boost other organizations' infrastructure and capacity, including that of mental health services providers and those offering wellness opportunities. Individual organizations approved in this grant had already provided some services and were now submitting invoices for their work, along with future programming ideas and strategies to assist the community. For instance, the Visiting Nurse Association wished to continue providing grief support services. The Resiliency Center of Newtown offered creative and alternative treatments such as art and music therapy. Newtown Youth and Family Services provided counseling and youth bureau programming. Each group was compensated for its important work. Yet in the eighteen months it took for the grant to be processed and money to be dispersed, local mental health providers doing the best they could to support the town's needs were consistently overwhelmed.

Newtown officials didn't have a support structure in place to adequately meet the community's needs. And why would they? A tragedy like this had never occurred before. New systems and procedures would be needed to address ongoing mental health issues in the community.

MY ROLE

On the day of the shooting, I watched the news unfold just like millions of other people. The difference was that Newtown was only thirty minutes from my home. At the time, I was working as the behavioral health director for Catholic Charities of Fairfield, Connecticut, a nonprofit organization that also served the Newtown area. As soon as we heard about the shooting, we began to strategize about ways our organization could provide support.

The next day, as I was preparing to go to my psychotherapy office, I received a call from a psychiatrist who worked closely with me at Catholic Charities. She had a personal request: a close friend who had lost a son in the shooting needed help. The family had four other children, and the two youngest, one a twin of the son who was killed, hadn't yet been told that their brother was not coming home. The parents needed guidance and assistance in breaking the news. I asked for a few minutes to cancel appointments with clients; then I would go to their house to provide whatever assistance I could.

I spent the next four hours working with the family in the most intimate way, not to make sense of what was happening, but simply to provide guidance on necessary and immediate steps to communicate the enormity of the loss to their children. This was the ultimate example of the clinical practice of holding space in a safe way while allowing the emotions of life to flow. The afternoon culminated with the family sitting together in their grief while the children were told that their brother had been killed at school.

Three months later, I saw these same parents at a recovery event in a neighboring state. The three day event had a lot of participant interaction. I did not want to trigger their pain, and did not know if they would be uncomfortable with my presence. That time I spent in their living room was heart wrenching and had created an indelible image in my mind of raw, inconsolable pain. Yet I put my reservations aside and decided to walk over to say hello. As I approached them, I extended my hand and said something like, "It's good to see you here." To my surprise, they looked at me in complete confusion. They had no idea who I was.

This is what trauma looks like and how deeply it affects the brain. Post-traumatic stress often results in cognitive and behavioral changes and deficits. Emotional flooding transfers into a breakdown in cognitive processing, including absent or diminished recall of the event and the most painful experiences connected to it. These parents were in the throes of trauma. In Newtown, most of the community had some variation of post-traumatic stress. And to make things more complicated, what one person may process as a life-altering interaction may be processed by another trauma victim as a numbing experience of which they have only foggy or minimal recall.

Over the next year and a half I went about my work at Catholic Charities and provided support to the Sandy Hook community whenever I could. This meant employing counselors for their Catholic school, securing grant money to provide clinical coverage to families and individuals affected by the tragedy at a nearby mental health center, and deploying therapists to offer support at events when asked.

CREATING A RECOVERY AND RESILIENCY TEAM

Once the DOJ grant was received, it was used to create the Newtown Recovery and Resiliency Team (NRRT). A colleague pushed me to apply for a Community Outreach Liaison position posted through the Town of Newtown. This person would be the de facto director of the NRRT. The job description was brief, and the listed expectations both vague and wide-ranging:

- Conduct long-term strategic planning, assessment, facilitations, coordination, training, vetting, and advocacy at a high level in the community
- Serve as the pivotal position in the community for residents, providers, funders, and municipal and community leaders to learn about available resources. This role will be the central position in Newtown responsible for monitoring and supporting the response efforts
- Help link service providers with available funds to stimulate community networking and build capacity to achieve identified core community objectives
- Facilitate discussion among all groups that have raised money in response to the tragedy to ensure each group shares its scope and mission in order to eliminate duplication and identify gaps
- Anticipate and respond to ever-changing community issues

This sounded interesting to me, but I was concerned the goals were too open-ended. How could anyone anticipate the ever-changing needs of a community in crisis? It wasn't until later on that I realized this disconnect was due to the fact that the grant was not written through a clinical lens, with guidelines to inform expectations and outcomes.

The lack of clarity in the description made me reluctant to apply, but something compelled me to send my resume in anyway, on the day before the posted deadline. I was called in for several interviews then and, to my surprise, was offered the position. Over the next few days, I searched for information on stepping into the realm of community recovery following a mass tragedy that is not due to a natural disaster. But there was little in the way of literature to provide guidance. I accepted the position even though I was uneasy. I knew I didn't have the specific expertise, but I could use my skillset as a clinician and nonprofit leader to assess and build recovery efforts. I accepted the challenge with the understanding that I had a year and a half to create meaningful results. The grant term was for just eighteen months.

Operating under a $400,000 budget, my team was tasked to create infrastructure, services, and best practices to meet the mental health needs of a highly-impacted community. Interestingly, the grant award was earmarked for recovery programming for the entire town, but no one seemed to recognize the immense emotional and organizational collateral damage to the broader community that we would have to navigate, address, and resolve. The grant offered only a basic outline for the work. The 2013 Needs Assessment—a survey on the emotional state of the town in the shooting's aftermath—was helpful. It identified who might be impacted and how to categorize their needs. But it did not provide a guide for the recovery process. My first task was to start at the beginning—get a comprehensive grasp of the community's current needs. It had been more than a year since the last town-wide assessment. From there, I could make better decisions about allocating time and resources.

I brought together a talented team of professionals and embarked on the project with aid from outside experts and dedicated community supporters. It was truly a collaborative effort as we navigated the turbulent waters of forging a model for healing a community. I strongly believe that the programs I set up and the lessons I learned can be applied to any community that faces these challenges.

Unfortunately for Newtown, the DOJ grant lacked a framework emphasizing trauma-informed care or clinical best practices. While restoring wellness and resiliency encompasses many realms of treatment and community effort, understanding complicated grief and trauma is vital to every healing service. Because this was not a focus before the NRRT was in place, it was an uphill battle to explain the importance and justify the cost of having trained, qualified professionals deliver programming. It also became important to spend time educating the public, town leaders, and local clinicians on trauma-informed approaches to care. The team constantly had to learn on the job, and at the same time set a precedent for the clinical response to community recovery.

In addition to bringing in outside experts on community recovery, trauma, and grief work, we partnered with the Newtown/Sandy Hook Community Foundation to provide assistance and funding. The foundation was born out of the tragedy; it managed most of the donations that flooded in and provided financial support for much of the individual clinical and wellness treatments, as well as grants for programming that enhanced recovery.

While our team developed an array of recovery programming, we also supported efforts by local foundations, organizations, and faith-based institutions to educate and assist the community, and included these programs in our resource repertoire. Finally, we were tasked to continue work previously assumed by the State Office of Victim Services, which encompassed assessments to reimburse individuals impacted by the tragedy in need of financial assistance. While this part of the job was not anticipated, it was a natural fit for our comprehensive case management.

My team had to formulate a plan for parents, students, and first responders. Not only was every subsection of the community in a different stage with different needs, but every individual within each subgroup was also in a different stage with different needs. Trauma-related wounds are easy to reopen. A triggering event, such as news of another incident, the anniversary of the tragedy, back-to-school season, or a lockdown drill, would often require the therapeutic process to start anew even if the individual was making significant progress.

Newtown's recovery was further complicated by a number of issues. The maze of finding and connecting its most vulnerable population— the children—to mental health resources daunted the families and their medical providers. They also had to navigate the immediate presence of media, the young age of victims, the rural location of the town, the violent nature of the crime, the tragedy having occurred at their school, an overwhelming influx of donated goods, and political issues that fractured groups. Challenges to a traumatized community are on a continuum of evolving needs impacted by culture, other world events, community resources, finances, geographic location, local leadership, media attention, socioeconomic status, the number and age of victims, the site of the actual tragedy, the trauma having been inflicted by a person, and the background and motive of the perpetrator.

The NRRT inherited a community generously supported by donations and endowed with wonderful grassroots organizations, yet Newtown was still fractured on many levels. One confounding factor was the decision on how resources should be allocated. At first there was an abundance of financial support with new foundations and means to service those impacted. But even the outpouring of money created fissures and a need for enhanced sensitivity, management, and independent oversight.

Another factor was the strong personal beliefs and political divides that surfaced due to the nature of the tragedy—issues such as gun control versus mental health advocacy and treatment. Did the tragedy stem from a lack of responsibility or awareness? There were many sources of information, yet few people were on the same page.

Worst of all, though, was the tremendous pain caused by conspiracy theorists who insisted that the tragedy was staged. Multiple blogs and YouTube videos promoted the lie that the shooting was put on by actors portraying grieving families. Many of the victims' loved ones, as well as parents and children who survived the shooting, were harassed by conspiracy theorists. To have families violently torn apart and portrayed as perpetrators of a hoax was unusually cruel. It further traumatized the victims, and created outrage in the community.

Newtown was also inundated with well-intentioned "helpers"— later termed "SUVs" (spontaneous uninvited visitors). What was lacking was collaboration among high-level management and clear pathways to services. Without a plan to manage these factors, confusion ensued, and we were dropped in the middle of it all.

The sudden international notoriety continued to compound these issues and act as its own layer of difficulty. The steady presence of media, curiosity seekers, and uninvited helpers intruded on the privacy of Sandy Hook School staff, students, and families, and in the weeks and months that followed the shooting, hindered the ability of residents to move freely through town or return to normal life.

I was always aware that our work took place in the infancy stages of Newtown's healing, and that a community trauma of this magnitude would require a recovery system available for the next ten to fifteen years. The NRRT operated for twenty-one months in total (we were granted a small extension), and our experiences and the lessons we learned are recorded in this book.

In the end, I did not leave the position feeling triumphant. How could I, after dealing with complicated grief, widespread trauma, and families whose lives had been torn apart? Yet I was proud of our accomplishments and honored to have had a small part in providing pathways to individual and family healing.

Little did I know that future tragedies would be both numerous and massive in proportion. Across the US and around the world, many communities have found themselves torn apart following a shooting, bombing, or other destructive act of violence. Since Newtown's tragedy, we have turned on the news to hear of massacres at schools, churches, nightclubs, concerts, movie theaters, shopping malls, restaurants, marathons, military bases, businesses, and on city streets.

WHAT THIS BOOK CAN DO

As the director of the Newtown Recovery and Resiliency Team, I was tasked with creating a response to the consequences of the Sandy Hook School shooting. My work was influenced by my direct experiences, as well as the best approaches for treating complicated grief and trauma. This book is meant to pass on this knowledge while addressing the needs of individuals and the targeted subgroups that comprise a community. It is my greatest hope that the structure and programs we developed can be sustained beyond my team's presence and applied to similar situations. While there is no plan that would fit every community, our story provides a model that can be duplicated, adjusted, or enhanced. In the smallest sense, it offers a place to start—guidance and clarity to this messy work. But I also hope it provides a method to create infrastructure ahead of time so that when tragedy does strike, your community is prepared.

Twenty-one months did not allow us to collect enough hard data for a research study, but the valuable, hands-on knowledge we gained—regarding what works and what doesn't when dealing with grief and trauma on a large scale—may become part of the template for disaster planning. For instance, we learned many lessons about the importance of engagement: that there is no substitute for meeting people where they are, that many individuals require nontraditional treatments, and that often a layered therapeutic approach is required. We developed programs to educate people on the concept of existential trauma—complex phases that transform a community after a tragedy of this magnitude. We identified effective treatment modalities that focused on brain-based strategies and whole body healing. We gained firsthand knowledge of the financial impact traumatized individuals suffer and the role money plays in a healing process, and we developed plans to assess future financial needs to cover community treatment and support. We learned that communication is tricky at best and carries a heavy burden.

Overall, we encountered obstacles, but ultimately we accumulated the knowledge and experience to overcome them, and can now predict the immense challenges other communities will face recovering from devastating loss.

Our model combined intimate individual assistance, small- and large-scale education, and training. This unique mix of services was critical to our success.

HOW THIS BOOK IS STRUCTURED

I've divided *Healing a Community* into two sections. Part I addresses large-scale concepts that are applicable to any community recovering from a crisis of mass proportion. Chapter One explains the initial assessment that identified the affected communities and informed our overall plan; recovery work cannot begin without a defined scope and target recipients. Chapter Two analyzes trauma from a clinical-based lens; while there are many resources for trauma care guidance and strategies, this chapter provides insight into the concept as it relates to an entire community. Chapter Three outlines the process of building a recovery team and system that emphasizes the collaborative approach. Chapter Four explains the concept of comprehensive care coordination, which is fundamental to assess and deliver all-inclusive mental health services. Chapter Five is a window into the unexpected challenges in recovery work, including the politics of recovery; it also takes a look at how community leaders may be impacted by their trauma exposure, and how this can influence recovery work. Chapter Six focuses on finances, since funding a recovery project can be an overwhelming undertaking; this chapter provides an understanding of how money influences the quality and quantity of the work.

Part II provides an individualized lens, highlighting specific approaches and strategies for treating different subsets of the community. Recovery can never be a one-size-fits-all approach. This section illustrates successful programs that the NRRT developed, and allows the reader to gain a greater understanding of the need to engage individuals and groups where they are. Chapter Seven is a snapshot of trauma-based therapies and programs that successfully delivered both immediate and sustainable relief to those who were suffering. Chapter Eight focuses on the delicate work of providing support to families that have lost loved ones. Chapter Nine delves into the unique needs of survivors of trauma, including individuals who were on site when the tragedy occurred. Chapter Ten outlines a successful program for first responders, and the nuances of working within this group's culture. Chapter Eleven provides ideas to help other support-givers in the community, such as clergy, mental health clinicians, and pediatricians. Chapter Twelve explains the vital role self-care plays in recovery. And finally, Chapter Thirteen looks at what we didn't have a chance to accomplish. Community recovery is a long-term endeavor—the changes suffered by the community are indelible and will likely require attention for years. A recovery team has a responsibility to identify future needs and inform local leaders in their forecasts for funding, positions, and ongoing assistance.

PART I

Parsing Community Needs

CHAPTER ONE

IDENTIFYING AFFECTED COMMUNITIES

The recovery process begins by first identifying whom you will serve: the web of people inside the community who need mental health services. Knowing the populations that may be impacted in advance is one of the primary ways a municipality can prepare for future disasters; you cannot simply wait to see whom walks in the door. Although you will find that there is a continual fluidity, and will likely re-evaluate the work as time goes by, defining who to focus on and what boundaries to set will dictate the programming, team makeup, and services you provide. Recovery is already a complicated undertaking, so having a strong sense of whom you are there to serve is vital as you communicate your mission and explain the scope of the work to the community.

If you proceed without establishing such clarity, you are likely to find that both your staff and the public will be confused about what you mean to accomplish. Remember that you will work within a traumatized environment, which breeds confusion and chaos in and of itself. For instance, before I set up the Newtown Recovery and Resiliency Team (NRRT) office, many people in the Newtown community had already begun to view outside "helpers" with caution, anger, and resentment. They had met with many mental health providers who made exaggerated claims about their own expertise and what their roles would be going forward. In the end, many of these providers left town, leaving unfulfilled promises and individuals still in crisis in their wake. However, when my team made it clear whom we were meant to serve with a unified message, even though the plan allowed for some flexibility, the public embraced our work with trust.

In identifying your target audience, you may need to defer to the dictates of local politicians or grant providers. In the aftermath of a community tragedy, there are always many voices with differing opinions and agendas. For example, I heard from many Newtown residents who believed that the NRRT's services should focus solely on individuals who lost a family member or were in the school and witnessed the shooting. I knew, however, that the grant we worked under did not read that way.

The NRRT was born out of a Department of Justice Consequence Management Phase II grant. The initial premise of the grant was for the Town of Newtown to form an assessment team to assist in developing and implementing short- and long-term strategic planning on a community-wide level. The primary function of the NRRT was to open a direct-access site housing all of our services—care coordination, trauma treatment, assessments for financial reimbursement, and the development of education and support programs for the entire Newtown community.

This is at least how I interpreted the grant. But because it was the first of its kind to address community recovery, we were in uncharted waters.

In any case, the creation of the NRRT was a small component of the entire Consequence Management Grant. The $7 million fund was also earmarked to support local organizations' programming and build up the capacity of existing infrastructure (such as the expanded services at a local youth organization, additional grief support groups from the visiting nurse association, and new security personnel for all schools). Because the grant was not written from a clinical perspective, the $420,000 set aside for the NRRT was supposed to cover salary and infrastructure costs—not clinical treatment. It defined our clientele as the entire town, which was officially designated a Victim of Crime. This meant every Newtown resident—approximately 28,000 individuals of all ages—could potentially request our services. What's more, the general public was never shown the grant language; it was not printed in the newspaper or posted online on the town government's website. This lack of transparency meant Newtown residents were left to make up their own minds on how that money should be used. The only information they had came from newspaper stories highlighting the fact the town had received $7 million of federal aid.

This information gap caused many problems for us. For instance, there was no grant money to cover outside care (that funding would come from a local foundation), but there was a pervasive misconception that federal money was available for individual services. Part of my job was to make sure grant money was spent properly. However, by the time I came on board much of the earmarked funds had already been spent in anticipation of its approval, since services had been needed and the grant was not approved until eighteen months after the shooting. Many of those services were still needed, in fact, and organizations struggled to raise additional funds to meet the town's ongoing needs. My team was hired and ready to start, yet no grant money was allocated for us to provide mental health programming. Suddenly, if I wanted to bring in an expert for a community-wide program, I had to find new sources of financial support.

THE RIGHT WAY TO WRITE A GRANT

I believe a grant of this size, when meant to address the consequences of a community tragedy, should have an emphasis on fulfilling three components, including expected outcomes for:

- Safety and security
- Psychoeducation and training
- Clinical recovery response

The perfect grant should be written in consultation with a clinical mental health provider, with precise language, and from a trauma-informed perspective that influences every aspect of the recovery plan—from the site specifics to the vetting of staff, funds for programming, and the expectations of organizations receiving money. A clinical perspective would recognize the need to cover mental health care and coordination, not simply the operating budget. It would suggest best practice models for treatment, understand the layers of care needed for healing, and anticipate an appropriate timeframe to address all aspects of recovery.

Our grant funded many types of mental health services; however, there was no consistency to best practice treatment approaches or standards of care. And while the grant may have identified perceived needs, in many areas it fell short concerning the specialized services required to address those specific needs. This created challenges. For instance, the grant correctly identified that a first responder recovery programming may be needed, but the funding provided for that service was inadequate to apply the appropriate model.

Our grant did not have a clear exit strategy, either. When the monies were gone and timeframes complete, there was little thought as to what would come next. This created tense discussions and meetings. It was difficult to impress upon town leadership the need for ongoing clinical recovery work, because that was not in the grant's original scope and it would have been costly to support. Ideally, programming would have continued beyond the NRRT's expiration date. Instruction to collect data on those we served, in order to inform the community of potential future needs for mental health, wellness, and recovery services, would also have helped.

CREATE A TOWN-WIDE MENTAL HEALTH BASELINE WHEN TRAGEDY STRIKES

Trauma of this magnitude can bring an individual's old, unresolved personal issues to the surface—an ongoing drug or alcohol issue, a fractured marriage, financial stress, and more. Understanding the overall health of your community before a tragedy can help you map the trauma trajectory. The best way to capture this information after a crisis, though, is through an immediate town-wide survey.

A survey serves two purposes: it helps to define who you will service and what they need. Your community might have preliminary information collected from previous surveys, and that is a valid place to start. I started with the community needs assessment completed by the Newtown/Sandy Hook Community Foundation six months after the tragedy. Their questionnaire was sent via email and regular mail to all Newtown residents to set a baseline for where the community was in terms of individual recovery. This survey was conducted one year before I came onboard, and it provided the following information:

- The number of people who reported a substance abuse issue before the tragedy
- The number of people who were struggling financially before the tragedy
- The number of people who were having marriage difficulties before the tragedy
- The number of people who were receiving mental health treatment before the tragedy

The survey also informed on what individuals and families felt were areas in need of prioritizing and gaps in services.

Knowing this information allowed me to set our mission and decide where to focus our time and money. A survey can be utilized several times through the course of recovery work. It can inform your decisions about mental health needs. It can alert you to trends and services that are less effective. It may suggest the best ways to communicate with the community, and more.

Because the grant's language was vague and the survey results dated, I decided that we needed a new assessment to carefully define who we were going to service and what would ultimately be provided. My survey also went to all residents, but it included more questions to determine the kinds of services we needed to provide.

There is tremendous value in allowing for community input. I believe this was integral to our acceptance in the community. Residents felt that they were making their own care decisions rather than having those choices made for them or imposed upon them. It helped to avoid the issue of people saying, "How do you know what we need? You're not walking in our shoes."

There are several factors to consider when developing a survey. Remember, you are working with a traumatized community. You may have to deliver the survey a few different ways in order to reach the most individuals and assure accurate responses, such as via email using Survey Monkey, through the postal service, and phone solicitation. Also consider the following:

- Will it be anonymous or allow for people to identify themselves?
- Who should assist in collecting the data?
- How will it be scored and/or interpreted?
- Will you use a Likert Scale for responses?
- Will participants complete the survey as individuals, families, or both?

Your survey questions target the need for education, support, assessment, referral, access to services, resource identification, and engagement. Engagement means asking how someone would like to receive information about events and programs, which formats for programming they would most likely participate in, and what barriers exist to attending events or programs (e.g., transportation, daycare, work schedule). In some communities you might need to include questions about language barriers or a lack of resources to receive information.

WHAT OUR SURVEY TOLD US

Through survey results and conversations with town officials, we were able to plan in an educated and informed way. The information showed clear gaps in service needs. This was to be expected; the nature of community recovery is such that through time, needs evolve. What the community needed in the event's immediate aftermath was different from what it needed two years later. More people had begun expressing a need for assistance, either because their awareness of the emotional and physical impact had heightened, or because there was increased public knowledge of potential services available. The survey also indicated that the tragedy's impact had rippled further than originally anticipated.

We learned that the need for services extended well beyond the Sandy Hook School community. If you do a strong job educating the public about trauma, and spread awareness about the services you provide, more people will come forward asking for help.

Although we started our work by identifying some of the immediately impacted groups that were surveyed in the initial community needs assessment, we expanded our treatment range as we went along. Eventually, we came to define the community for our scope of service delivery to include all those who identified themselves as impacted, as well as those who we knew had some level of trauma. Sandy Hook School personnel received their own grant money for recovery services from the Department of Education, which meant our outreach was not meant to address their needs. However, several school personnel still reached out to our office for help. Because we defined our work as encompassing the entire community, I argued that these individuals were still included, and we should open our services to them as long as there was no duplication of service. While this ruffled some feathers, it allowed us to move forward with consistency and strength.

CRISIS VS. CONSEQUENCE MANAGEMENT

Community disasters are typically managed in distinct phases. In Sandy Hook, the grant divided the experience into Phase I, "the crisis management phase," and Phase II, "the consequence management phase." A crisis phase includes the tragedy itself, the immediate response, and the initial assessment. It involves securing the crime scene, delivering reports on the tragedy, and setting up a crisis response to stabilize the community. The duration of the crisis phase will change depending on the type of disaster you are dealing with. Every organization involved in recovery work may define the crisis stage differently. If there is a shooting, the crisis phase can last through the final funeral, the return to school and work life, and the waning presence of the media. In a natural disaster, the crisis phase can continue through the cleanup effort or through securing housing and basic needs for those displaced.

The consequence management phase is when you address the emotional needs of the community once it resumes some semblance of normal life. The impact of a disaster on the fabric of the community becomes most apparent when the media moves out and the rest of the world moves on, schools are reopened, people go back to work, and the bodies have been buried, their stories told.

In our DOJ grant, the understanding was that Newtown was well past its crisis phase, and the consequence phase would only last for the next eighteen months. But as we assessed the community needs it became apparent that this timeframe was wholly inadequate. We now know the consequences of events like Sandy Hook are far-reaching and long-term. What's more, there is no clear way to predict when the consequence phase will end. I can confidently say that Newtown's community needs will extend for many years beyond the initial event, and several years past the disbandment of our recovery team.

Sometimes it was difficult to explain this notion to town leaders. It was hard for them to understand that people four or five steps removed from the tragedy were also struggling, and that their needs were not going to completely dissipate after the initial recovery response. Community trauma and grief is both a collective and personal experience, which further complicates the healing process. Recovery efforts need to be delivered on both the group and individual levels.

This may mean extending assistance well beyond your initial scope of service. It's not hard to imagine that the neighbor of a child who passed away might be severely impacted. Or a boy who lost two friends on his soccer team. Or a babysitter who looked after one of the young victims. The person who teaches a class at the gym, a mailman, townspeople who watched the media descend on their neighborhoods, seeing on television what was happening while they were just blocks away—they too might have been impacted by the shooting.

As is the case in most small towns, the families of Sandy Hook were interconnected through their neighborhoods, schools, children's activities, religion, sports, and work. These relationships were often the key to emotional support and resilience, but also multiplied the number of individuals whose functioning was impaired by the tragedy. It often seemed to us that those ripples expanded every day. However, in actuality the ripples were not growing; the number of people who felt comfortable coming forward for assistance was rising.

IDENTIFYING WHO IS IMMEDIATELY AFFECTED: THE CRISIS PHASE

How well the crisis phase is managed may dictate how smoothly the transition to the consequence phase goes. If residents feel that they are receiving accurate and up-to-date information from trustworthy leaders, they will be more likely to embrace the healers and access help. Yet if there are gaps in communication, confusion about where to seek answers, a sense of division among residents, frustration, insecurity, and resentment, a feeling of helplessness can pervade.

Taking care of the needs of those who were closest to the tragedy makes sense, and these cases are easy to identify. In the crisis phase, an accurate assessment of those impacted will begin with the total number of people most closely impacted. For instance, in Newtown, the 2013 assessment helped identify the needs and gaps for service provision. Town leaders identified that the victims' parents and families, the 458 students enrolled at the Sandy Hook School and their families, the ninety-one members of the Sandy Hook School staff, as well as the first responders, were all considered to be the residents most closely impacted. The assessment also showed that the ripples of affected individuals went far beyond those survivors and their families. Even the definition of "first responders" came up for debate. The surviving school personnel at Sandy

Hook believed they were the true first responders, while most others in town identified the first responders as the police and emergency medical services (EMS) staff that had rushed to the scene. In truth, both groups were clearly impacted, but they required different types of intervention.

During the crisis phase, the following groups of individuals were identified as likely to require mental health services:

- Families who lost a child or adult family member in the shooting
- Children who were inside the school at the time of the shooting
- The forty staff members and students who directly witnessed the shooting
- Families of children who were inside the school at the time of the shooting
- Students and families of students enrolled in other schools in the district
- Sandy Hook School personnel who were inside the building during the shooting
- Emergency medical services providers who were on the scene
- Local hospital triage staff
- The medical examiner's staff
- Connecticut state police
- Newtown police

When we started working in the community, we realized that additional groups should have been included as people immediately affected during the crisis phase. Some examples were:

- Local medical practitioners
- Bus drivers working at the Sandy Hook School
- Gravediggers
- Funeral directors
- Town employees
- Clergy
- Mental health clinicians who worked with those impacted

IDENTIFYING WHO IS AFFECTED: THE CONSEQUENCE PHASE

The NRRT was formed specifically to address the consequence phase, because the town realized treatment gaps had been left unfilled during the crisis phase. The assumption was that we would address a population similar to the one seen during the crisis phase, but in reality the web of affected individuals had continued to grow exponentially. Many different groups were not initially serviced, even though their needs were great. We managed to identify some of these groups and create appropriate treatment and programming options. But during the consequence phase it is impossible to fully predict the number or type of impacted individuals who will walk through your door seeking help.

There might also be groups who are identified as having needs, but are in denial or resist participating for fear of exposing their vulnerabilities. For instance, six months into our work, the clinicians providing mental health services needed support themselves to address vicarious traumatization. We also learned that in the culture of first responders and emergency personnel, it's common to avoid acknowledging your vulnerabilities in order to carry out ongoing job functions without distraction.

In the consequence phase, you will begin to identify people who were not at the scene at all but associate physical and emotional changes with the tragedy. For us, this included:

- Spouses and loved ones of Sandy Hook School staff
- Families of Newtown area students
- Babysitters/caretakers of surviving students
- Residents who lived near the school
- Residents who lived near the perpetrator
- Residents who lived near victim families
- People who went to the emergency shelter firehouse on the day of the tragedy
- Family members of first responders

We also heard from individuals who were not Newtown residents, yet felt affected by the tragedy. Some were connected to it through work in town. Others felt impacted through extended family, or as friends and colleagues of people killed. As I spent time with key town leaders, I learned that municipal employees were also in need of support. They had remained helpless at their jobsites as the news unfolded. We ended up working with people in many town departments, as well as staff from other schools in the district.

DEVELOPING YOUR SCOPE OF SERVICES

After you've identified your target constituents, set about developing your scope of services. To do this, there are several questions you'll need to consider:

- Are you in an urban area where treatment resources may be plentiful, or a rural area where resources are scarce? You may need to devote a significant amount of time to recruiting resources. Or, if they are in abundance, you'll need to vet the quality and accessibility of those existing services.

- What is the demographic makeup of your community? Will you need to hire a culturally diverse staff? The Orlando nightclub shooting is an example of this. I imagine they needed to recruit bilingual, Hispanic clinicians as well as those skilled in LGBTQ-related issues.

- What is the socioeconomic makeup of your community? Will funds be a primary concern for many, or will money not be an issue? Will you need to dedicate and train staff to navigate the insurance arena? Will you need to work with the state to assist individuals in obtaining coverage?

- Did the tragedy involve children, or just adults? Will you need child-specific services?

- What services are being provided by other entities? Are people satisfied with these services? And who has a stake in their success? For instance, there may be other grants that have been awarded, expanding the capacity of existing organizations that now depend on service provision for financial support. There may also be subsets of the impacted communities that receive exclusive funding or service provision for their smaller community.

- Did the immediate, direct result of the tragedy primarily involve emotional trauma, or physical trauma as well? This may indicate a need for medically based resources and/or dedicated staff that have a medical background to inform this arena. It may also indicate the need to work closely with state disability professionals.

- What, if any, financial compensation was provided to assist those impacted to date? What is the mechanism to assess and pay out this money? Will you be involved? Money is a key component to the recovery process. Are there adequate resources, or will you need to bring awareness to funding concerns and help raise more money?

- Are your community leaders ready to assist in the recovery process? Who are they? If there are well-respected leaders who bring clout with their support for recovery efforts, they will be invaluable. If not, you will likely need to devote energy to educating and gaining support from your community leaders, or at least to minimizing the downplaying of your efforts.

Our second community needs assessment survey indicated that my team needed to act as a liaison between the town's clinical school staff and existing mental health and health and wellness providers. Throughout the development of your recovery work, it is vitally important that you create trusting relationships with the community at large. You do not want to duplicate existing services and programs, and you do not want to step on the toes of local organizations in the recovery realm. We learned this the hard way. It is a delicate balance to express that you are here to fill in gaps and deliver recovery services without making those who already provide services feel as though they have somehow fallen short, or are being minimized. While you may have been hired as an expert in your field, you still have to show respect to, and value the work of, the practitioners who arrived before you. If those groups are going to continue their work, you want to collaborate with them wherever possible. Always try to make others see you as an asset to them. We realized, though, that the town's providers were not adequate in number or training, and had to look further for appropriate programs and care.

We set out to create trusting relationships with the community at large, prioritizing school staff and families, and then reached out to the special populations. For the full community, we provided education, support, assessment, referrals, access to services, resource identification, and engagement. There was also a distinct need for education about trauma, grief, and clinical "self-care" support. This makes sense. When existing groups are deployed to a crisis, there is often no time to assess gaps in training, or consider their own support needs.

Following the second community needs assessment, we made a timeline to chart how we would deliver services to the broader affected communities. We established an individualized approach while formulating comprehensive programs for different groups based on access or needs. Some programs would continue for a full year, such as one we created for the town's police department. Others were grouped as a series of educational events. We also launched a support group for area mental health providers to review cases and discuss ongoing issues, concerns, and struggles.

Finally, as we faced the final stages of our work nearly four years after the initial incident, we continued to see individuals who had never sought assistance before suddenly reach out for help. At first, some couldn't explain how the shooting had impacted them, but they knew their lives had felt different since it occurred. Four years is still the infancy stage for recovery from massive trauma. I believe we were instrumental in increasing education and awareness, expanding access to best practice resources, creating dialogue on needs and support, and forging collaborative inroads to individual and community wellness.

It is important to note that this scope may evolve many times during your work. As you continue to assess needs, and the community builds trust in your ability to provide quality assistance, you will be surprised by who walks in the door, and this should be viewed as a sign that you have established a positive reputation and rapport. Remember, a key characteristic needed for successful recovery work is flexibility. The needs of each individual and family are inherently unique. As you peel back the layers of an issue, you will often find several more that are neglected or repressed. A marriage that is unhealthy but holding on by a thread may truly unravel when exposed to a traumatic event. A department with long-standing unaddressed management issues will often splinter under the stress of responding to a tragedy. An individual who hides a substance abuse problem from family and coworkers may no longer be able to maintain that secrecy. A parent with existing financial stressors can be tipped over the edge by new therapy bills, or quit work because she has been greatly impacted by trauma and no longer functions optimally. The individual who experienced trauma firsthand may now be unable to be present for his family; he may be "checking out," losing his temper, or crying all the time. An individual who enjoyed a fairly predictable lifestyle may feel compelled to leave that security and join a social or political movement, neglecting other responsibilities. A parent may become so overprotective it erodes her relationship with her spouse.

Understand the need to make distinctions in your approach to group programming as well. We learned quickly that each impacted subset has different mental health service needs, just as every traumatized individual will be at a different place in their recovery process. First responders require different programming than clinicians, clinicians require different programming than parents, and parents require different programming than clergy. This was true for obvious reasons: culture, community expectations, level of trauma exposure, the ability to be open and vulnerable in the context of their roles, existing support structures, etc. Lots of underlying workplace issues that had nothing to do with mental health came to the surface following Newtown's tragedy: long-standing challenges within a hierarchy, union constraints, perceptions of how staff were treated in the immediate aftermath, a lack of support from those they expected support from, a feeling of being devalued or undermined, a need to appear in full control of their emotions, a lack of funds, feeling overworked and overwhelmed, receiving false guidance, etc.

The way to create effective approaches and programs is to be thoughtful and patient in the engagement process. Many times this means seeking outside guidance on the cultural nuances of each group, and hiring peers to assist with both engagement and the delivery of services. I had to learn the language of each group, meet them where they were, and above all not promise to fix all their long-standing issues.

IN SUMMARY

If you are establishing protocols for potential tragedies that have not occurred, leave the question of defining the community and services you will provide open-ended. However, the more information you can glean about your town before disaster strikes, the easier it will be to implement recovery work. This process is ever evolving, so you should also continuously assess needs and the efficacy of services. It's always important to hear firsthand from the community. I surveyed Newtown residents at several points, including midway through our assignment and at the end. We created an atmosphere of safety for individuals and groups to openly discuss their needs. Our programming was both influenced and enhanced by this feedback.

CHAPTER TWO

DEFINING TRAUMA AND COMPLICATED GRIEF

A traumatic event can change the very belief system of the individuals who are directly influenced, as well as hundreds more in the community just through vicarious exposure. In order to deliver the best practices of care, prepare your team to provide everyone in the community with information on the benefits of working with trained professionals, including the importance of incorporating specialized interventions to reduce distress and strengthen coping skills. It is also critical to educate everyone in the community, from its leaders to anyone impacted by a communal tragedy, on the emotional, physiological, and neurobiological consequences of trauma.

Educational programming on post-traumatic stress reactions is at the core of your effort. Without this knowledge, affected individuals may spend time spinning their wheels and wondering why they are not getting better, due to unrealistic expectations about what recovery looks like. Recovery and resilience is not a return to how you felt before the incident. It is moving through the trauma and grief, finding an acceptable and healthy way to resume your life without being consumed by adverse symptoms. This is one of the many reasons why having trained clinicians who are well versed in trauma and complicated grief is crucial to any recovery team.

The better you are at recognizing the signs and symptoms, the more likely you will deliver excellent care. However, this information is not the panacea many are looking for. I know firsthand that it's not easy to deliver this message. Talking about long-lasting pain and devastation can sound negative rather than hopeful. However, when you are fluent in the language of trauma, you can add that it may be even more damaging to convey the false hope that everyone is going to be better soon.

I was invited to many strategic planning meetings with representatives from the town as well as the federal government (officials from the Department of Education, for example), and these meetings rarely included discussions about trauma—what it looked like and how it affected the community. I was asked the same questions month after month: *Aren't people getting better? We're almost two years out. Things are moving on. Right? The need for services should be decreasing, correct? At this point people need to start taking responsibility for their own wellness.* It might be the instinct of political leaders to think this way; they are used to propping up constituents by delivering a positive message. Had they really understood the depth and scope of trauma in the aftermath of a tragedy, they would have responded differently. Instead, their best intentions came across as dismissive, and at times created a sense of fracturing.

Fracturing was a term we heard quite often in the Sandy Hook community. It referred to the fact that everyone was not on the same page. Perspectives and agendas differed on a myriad of issues, ranging from who was impacted, to where efforts and funds should be targeted, who could be trusted, how to memorialize the victims, and what should constitute security. When people felt like they were ignored or their pain was left unaddressed, it harbored a sense of isolation instead of a feeling of community recovery.

Recovery specialists must be skilled in detecting those reactions and provide resources and clinical strategies that encompass mind-body approaches to recovery. Yet you will be surprised by the lack of knowledge surrounding trauma and complicated grief, even within the clinical community. Many counselors are not trauma-informed therapists. In the communities in which they work they haven't had the need to be, but in these changing times, they do. Post-Traumatic Stress Disorder (PTSD) has become part of the common parlance. The diagnosis of PTSD was originally reserved for war veterans, but today we know that anyone exposed to a traumatic event who exhibits a marked change in their mind and body is suffering from PTSD.

Doing recovery work without an ability to recognize the impact of trauma can damage the individual. Imagine being told to stick with a treatment that has been ineffective, or hearing that you need to share your story in a support group even though the idea of doing so sends you into a state of depression and isolation. Imagine having self-destructive urges, wanting to cut yourself, drink, or gamble to quiet your anxiety, believing that's the only thing you can do to not feel powerless. And no amount of talking about your feelings changes that.

We might take some encouragement, however, by the number of heads nodding in agreement in a room full of people who identify with the language of trauma during an explanation of how the brain experiences a traumatic event. My team would often hear sighs of relief and see expressions of "Oh my God. That's why I feel the way I do. Why didn't someone explain this sooner?" That was a sign to me that we were making a real difference in these people's recovery a full two years after the incident. Unfortunately for many, it was the first time they had experienced relief.

THE BIOLOGY OF TRAUMA

Emotional and psychological trauma can result from extraordinarily stressful events that shatter one's sense of security, leaving an individual feeling helpless in a dangerous world. Unfortunately, this has become all too commonplace in our communities. While there will never be a return to the old normal, true resilience can take place, though it may take in excess of ten years to solidify. During that time period, each individual's brain is slowly rewiring. Here's how the initial trauma and the recovery period change one's biology.

The hypothalamus, which is the central access point of the brain, directs the central nervous system during stress. The brain and body house a complicated autonomic nervous system (ANS), which regulates bodily functions beyond our conscious control, such as temperature, digestion, metabolism, breathing, and heartbeat. The ANS is divided into two parts or systems that serve different functions but have a complimentary relationship. The first part is the sympathetic nervous system (SNS), which is responsible for arousal: it is what mobilizes us or gives the signal that it is time to move or expend energy. The second part is the parasympathetic nervous system (PSNS), which is responsible for calming the body down and conserving energy.

When we are faced with danger, the hypothalamus releases stress chemicals. These chemicals are transported to the adrenal gland, which becomes stimulated and produces stress hormones in increased amounts. This in turn activates our nervous system. The SNS automatically starts up without conscious thought, producing large amounts of the brain chemical adrenaline, which is accompanied by an increase in blood pressure or heart rate, rapid breathing, sweating, and spontaneous movement—the fight-or-flight response. When that stress or threat subsides, the PSNS kicks in and quiets the adrenaline production, returning the body to a restful state.

Emotional and psychological trauma can also evoke a similar response from the ANS. Experiences that involve psychological trauma shatter your sense of security, making you feel helpless and vulnerable in a world you perceive to be filled with danger and risk. Traumatic experiences often involve a threat to one's life or safety, but any situation that leaves you feeling overwhelmed and alone can be traumatic, even if it doesn't involve physical harm. It's not objective facts that determine whether an event is traumatic, but rather your subjective emotional experience of that event. The more frightened and helpless you feel, the more likely you are to be traumatized.

When trauma occurs, the SNS releases an excess of adrenaline, so that even after the threat is over and an individual's PSNS kicks in, he is left in a state of high alert. The more adrenaline floods the body, the greater the chance a temporary paralysis of the nervous system will occur. This produces a state of immobility: a freeze response. The trauma victim is in an altered state of reality in which time slows down. And while freezing may increase one's chances of survival, the trauma memory often gets stuck in the brain or body. The experience never gets erased, and a traumatized individual never completely resumes their previous level of functioning. Their vision of the world and how to navigate it changes forever.

The reaction loop of the SNS and PSNS continues, and the individual loses the ability to self-regulate emotions. This *dysregulation*, as it's called, manifests in a number of ways. An individual can look detached, unable to engage on a social level. Or he may find himself physically and emotionally reactive to any unpredicted stimuli. The individual can also develop an extreme sense of guilt that the freeze reaction took hold.

Until recently, we thought this was the extent of the damage that trauma could cause. Now we know exposure to a traumatic event affects physical health too, and can create lasting bodily harm. As trauma researcher Bessel Van der Kolk, MD, describes it: "Brain, body, and mind are inextricably linked. Alterations to one of these three will intimately affect the other two." An individual body expresses what cannot be verbalized. His groundbreaking work showed that trauma is stored in the brain and the body. Stephen Porges, PhD, further illustrates the mind-body translation of trauma exposure. His Polyvagal Theory looks beyond the fight-or-flight concept and highlights the direct relationship between stress and social and emotional behavior. The premise is that behaviors are manifested from survival actions suggested by the internal nervous system. And since we know that traumatic experiences can remain in the nervous system and emerge later in life, Porges' theory allows us to attach meaning to that experience and the resulting behavior. Instead of labeling adverse behaviors that result from remaining in an extreme state of mind following a traumatic experience (dysregulation, hyper-arousal, irritability, pervasive sadness, and detachment), we learn to understand the meaning and rationale behind these emotional and physical changes. This often leads to a greater ability to understand and treat these adverse reactions and unhealthy behaviors. When those suffering understand what their reactions and behaviors stem from, they can more easily connect with others and communicate thoughts and needs. Attaching words to the changes to one's nervous system is an important factor in healing.

Traumatic reactions are *normal* responses to *abnormal* situations. Imagine that you recently lived through a school shooting. You're in school again and hear a loud popping noise come from out of nowhere. Your immediate reaction is to run for cover. You find yourself screaming. Your brain is flooded with adrenaline released during the perceived threat. Your memory of the school shooting comes forward, the PSNS responds, and you instinctively hide under a desk. Later you feel embarrassed for having exposed your fear to others, but you still can't shake feeling unsafe for several agitating days, weeks, or months.

ASSESSING FOR TRAUMA

Following a traumatic event, or repeated trauma, people react in different ways, expressing a wide range of physical and emotional responses. There is no right or wrong way to think, feel, or behave, so don't judge your own reactions or those of others. Following exposure to a traumatic event, most individuals experience "temporary preoccupation"—involuntary intrusive memories. This is a variation in conscious thought and memory that is described often as a continuous re-living of the events surrounding the tragedy, such as a parent's last words to their child, the moment of being told a loved one did not survive, or the buzz of confusion and chaos while they waited for news of the outcome of the tragedy. This can appear as a new identity that takes hold. If it persists, it can turn into a constant re-victimization—a feeling that one can never get away from the association with the tragedy. In Sandy Hook, we witnessed symptomology including impulsive or unpredictable periods of dysregulation, expressions of "brain fogginess" that translated into numbness or disorganized thinking, extreme anxiety or panic, overthinking that resulted in a perceived lack of confidence or competency, irritability, a lack of awareness of social and emotional change, and lots of maladaptive behaviors to ease persistent feelings of distress.

When assessing for trauma, you need to get a clear picture of an individual's sense of internal regulation—how strong or fragile it might be. The reaction to traumatic pain is often expressed as frustration, fear, confusion, distrust, denial, pushback, and just plain raw emotion.

In Newtown we learned that after a devastating event the impact on the brain is such that even the individual's capacity for self-awareness is affected. Those around him see changes in personality and behavior, but he is unaware of the transformation. A person may present as highly agitated or completely detached. Someone capable of multi-tasking in the past may now be unable to organize her basic daily needs. A man who prided himself on his decision making and problem solving may now be unable to choose what to cook for dinner or whether to allow his child to go on a play date. Someone previously confident in her life choices may now question those decisions. Someone who felt overwhelmed prior to the tragedy may now be totally unable to support a family. A person inundated with caring for others may have sacrificed their own self-care. Some people may engage in unhealthy means of coping just to get through the day. Someone who relied on faith to carry him through difficult times before may walk away from his religion and feel isolated or lost. Someone who leaned on her spouse for strength in the past could feel that her partner has "checked out," or is on the brink of an emotional breakdown, so instead of gaining support from her partner she has a new source of stress. Someone living paycheck to paycheck might now be overwhelmed with medical bills, a concern that tips a daily stressor into thoughts of a bleak future. Someone who sent their children to school without a second thought before is now consumed with anxiety until the child returns home; this makes it difficult for the parent to get anything done.

Children react in their own unique ways. Some formerly confident high-achievers can suddenly feel unable to get through the day without support. Children who went to school without worrying about their home life may now fear for the well-being of their parents or siblings. Teachers who felt confident in the classroom before may now overthink every reaction or response, making the job exhausting and unmanageable. Individuals who used to get through each day with ease might now jump at every loud noise or opened door. A person once able to easily find joy in life may now be unable to feel happiness in anything.

Other emotional and psychological signs of trauma include:

- Anger, irritability, and mood swings
- Anxiety and fear (edginess, agitation)
- Confusion, difficulty concentrating
- Feeling sad, hopeless, and depressed

- Diminished problem-solving or coping skills
- Feeling disconnected or numb
- Guilt, shame, and self-blame
- Shock, denial, and disbelief
- Withdrawal from others

This is why traumatic memories often transform into physical outcomes. The longer a traumatized person lives without effective treatment, the more likely a host of physical, emotional, and mental disruptions to their functioning can become permanently embedded, including:

- Being easily startled
- Changes to eating patterns
- Changes to sleep patterns
- A compromised immune system (lingering colds or infections)
- Fatigue
- Headaches or migraines
- Irritable bowel symptoms/problems with digestion
- Muscle tension
- Nightmares/night terrors
- Racing heartbeat
- Spontaneous sweating
- Stomach aches

Because these changes are often subtle or meet other diagnostic criteria, if one is not trained to identify the trauma symptoms, it is easy to sweep them under the rug, believing they will dissipate on their own through time or with medication. For instance, it is easy to misinterpret maladaptive coping mechanisms as depression, anxiety, or an unwillingness to move forward.

Imagine if John Doe walks through the door of your recovery center. He says he doesn't even know why he is there, and that someone else can probably benefit more from the services than he will. He is tired all the time, and his wife said he needs help. A care coordinator begins her assessment and learns that John worked as a janitor in the school. He took pride in his work and became close to many of the students and staff. His school is now a crime scene, some students and staff are gone forever, and he wonders if somehow he could have done anything to prevent the tragedy or saved some of the people who were killed. It is nearly impossible to show up to work now and feel proud in his role. The weight of the tragedy hits him every time he walks in. John talks about how he used to feel competent and in control, but is now unable to focus, lacks the desire to work, has a short fuse with his kids and spouse at home, and suffers from continual low energy and an inability to experience pleasure. He is angry all the time, and he doesn't like his new self, but can't seem to look at the world without feeling resentment for what happened. He distances himself from friends, coworkers, and his family out of fear that his anger will cross the line into aggression. He used to turn to his faith for answers. Now he doesn't attend church. Drinking regularly is the only thing that calms his mind.

Or take Jane Smith, whose daughter was in the school the day of the shooting. She makes an appointment at the recovery center, walks in, and immediately becomes tearful, saying, "I can't make decisions anymore. When my kids ask if they can go to a friend's house after school, I can't answer them. I drop them off in the morning and sit in the parking lot unable to drive away. I can't decide what to make for dinner or how to complete a simple project at work. I cry all the time. I've gained weight and avoid going to the gym or any place where people know me and might expect something of me. And no one understands. Everyone around me acts as if I just need time to pull myself together. But I don't even know what that means or how to do it."

Upon assessment, the care coordinator learns that Jane's youngest of three children survived the school shooting. The child was in a classroom the shooter did not enter. However, another child on her daughter's soccer team, from a family she has spent many hours talking with on the sidelines, did not make it out of the school. The care coordinator begins to talk with these individuals about Post-Traumatic Stress Disorder. When we can identify these changes in thinking and behavior as a reaction to the trauma, the healing can begin.

The Anxiety and Depression Association of America offers the following diagnostic criteria for PTSD:

Exposure to actual or threatened death, serious injury, or sexual violence in one (or more) of the following ways:

1. Directly experiencing the traumatic event(s).
2. Witnessing, in person, the event(s) as it occurred to others.
3. Learning that the traumatic event(s) occurred to a close family member or close friend (cases of actual or threatened death must have been violent or accidental).

4. Experiencing repeated or extreme exposure to aversive details of the traumatic event(s) (e.g., first responders collecting human remains; police officers repeatedly exposed to details of child abuse).

The presence of one (or more) of the following intrusion symptoms associated with the traumatic event(s), beginning after the traumatic event(s) occurred:

1. Recurrent, involuntary, and intrusive distressing memories of the traumatic events. (In children older than six years, repetitive play may occur in which themes or aspects of the traumatic events are expressed.)

2. Recurrent distressing dreams in which the content or affect of the dream is related to the traumatic event(s). (In children, there may be frightening dreams without recognizable content.)

3. Flashbacks or other dissociative reactions in which the individual feels or acts as if the traumatic event(s) are recurring. Such reactions may occur on a continuum, with the most extreme expression being a complete loss of awareness of present surroundings. (In children, trauma-specific reenactment may occur in play.).

4. Intense or prolonged psychological distress at exposure to internal or external cues that symbolize or resemble an aspect of the traumatic event(s).

5. Marked physiological reactions to reminders of the traumatic event(s).

THE RETRIGGERING ASPECTS OF TRAUMA

Initial trauma symptoms and extreme feelings typically last from a few days to a few months, gradually fading as the individual processes the trauma. If these symptoms and feelings do not subside, we begin to discuss Post-Traumatic Stress Disorder. But even when someone reports feeling better, he may be troubled from time to time by painful memories or emotions, especially in response to triggers such as the incident's anniversary, or an image, sound, or situation that reminds him of the traumatic experience. The level of emotional balance versus dysregulation will vary for everyone; you never know who will be triggered by random, seemingly innocuous experiences or everyday events. Thoughts can become suddenly flooded with unwanted memories, which force an individual to revert back to feeling powerless, unsafe, angry, or numb.

I remember a former Sandy Hook schoolteacher entering the center with a frantic look of fear, her body shaking from head to toe. She explained that she heard police sirens coming from the area near the high school. We were just a few blocks from there, but no one in my office heard sirens. Then suddenly as she reported this, we did. This teacher had chosen to transfer to the district's middle school after the shooting because her emotions would not allow her to continue teaching at the elementary level. She had entered into therapy shortly after the tragedy, and was practicing self-care. She told us, "I thought I was okay. I thought I was doing everything right. But right now I feel like I'm losing my mind."

Our care coordinator and trauma specialist immediately helped her to scan her body so she could grasp where the re-traumatization had manifested. She said her heart was racing and she felt like she might stop breathing. The specialist introduced some tapping techniques, and the two practiced together—this helped her regain a sense of regulation in her body—and essential oils were presented to breathe in and reset the brain. Next, they worked on rhythmic breathing. Only after she had gained a sense of homeostasis did they begin to put a narrative to her sense of panic. If our staff had not understood the need to treat the body and regulate the nervous system, the therapist would likely have jumped into discussing this woman's feelings, which would have exacerbated her anxiety and panic.

HOW TO APPROPRIATELY RESPOND TO TRAUMA

Working with trauma involves specialized training to properly address the nervous system's upheaval and subsequent emotional impact. Recognizing the intricate ways in which trauma can change a person's belief system, sense of safety, life perspective, and lifestyle is the most important aspect of assisting in a constructive recovery path. The complexity involves many layers of individual and community perspective and is the reason why no two people experience the same path to recovery; history, culture, supports and resources, media presence, competent leaders and healers, preservation of safety, and disruption of basic needs all affect the healing trajectory.

When a person cannot go to a grocery store or pharmacy without being addressed as the parent of a child victim, her trauma remains in a reactive state. If someone must return to a teaching position without adequate time to heal, his trauma cannot be put to rest. When a caregiver returns to her role without addressing her own emotional needs, healthy coping skills are compromised. These are some reasons why I advocate for more specialized training for anyone who works with children and staff in school settings, particularly counselors, school nurses, and principals. Both lay and religious community leaders should also be trained to recognize trauma symptoms.

The role of the clinician is to initially help the individual transition to a state of regulation. This is where recovery begins. In regaining a sense of control over their body, the traumatized individual begins to feel less overwhelmed and more capable of moving forward. After assisting the transition to a state of regulation, the therapist should teach the individual strategies to practice self-regulation. When this is mastered, resilience can be achieved. The individual becomes aware of triggers and recognizes when their nervous system is aroused. When they are able to self-regulate, they can stay grounded through the triggering experience. Eventually, when they build a sense of competency in self-regulating, they may pass these skills on to others in the impacted community— from teacher to student, parent to child, individual to friend, and so on.

But when you work with a traumatized community, much of the information you share with patients doesn't get absorbed the first or second time you introduce it. As stated before, in a state of dysregulation their ability to process or retain new information is often impaired. You need to give the same instructions in many different ways. And none of it will be useful until the individual can learn to regulate his or her body. We had people describe feeling like their brains were in a fog, or admit that they struggled to organize information.

You should prepare to encounter challenging reactions to your recovery efforts from anyone in a trauma-affected community, including its leaders. Some may appear checked out, or need to step outside. Some may express resistance. Keep in mind that there is nothing personal about this response, even when it is directed toward you. There may be strong reactions to seemingly innocuous materials. You don't know what kind of landmines you might step on, or what could possibly trigger someone. When we ran programs, I had an extra staff member on hand just in case someone in the audience reacted acutely.

THE MIND-BODY APPROACH TO TRAUMA

One of the most transformative aspects of this work is helping people understand why they have felt different in their body since the traumatic event. When someone understands that the changes are the result of an impact to their brain and nervous system, it gives them permission to express vulnerability, fear, pain, guilt, and grief. Suddenly, there is recognition that the way they feel or think is not their fault, that they can't just wish it away, and that they are not going crazy. In the eighteen months I ran the NRRT, I can't tell you how many individuals looked at us with utter relief when we explained that their symptoms were common to trauma exposure, and that this was the brain's way of protecting them and making sense of what they had lived through.

After trauma, the mind is wired to sense danger and register fear the instant there might be a new threat. The result is a brain that is easily aroused at all times. Furthermore, when a seemingly inexplicable experience, like the massacre of children and educators in a school classroom, occurs at the hands of a mentally ill individual, the brain naturally tries to make sense of the event. But there is no coherent language to explain this outcome. The right and left sides of the brain, which are responsible for differing functions in our emotional and physical being, may become off-balance, and through the process of trying to make sense of the experience, the usual state of communication between the sides becomes chaotic or confused. The right side holds images, themes, and senses; the left side functions to make logical conclusions and put words to those feelings and perceptions held on the right side of the brain. The corpus callosum is the connector that allows these two halves to communicate—it's a bundle of nerves that integrates emotional and cognitive brain functions. But trauma creates an assault on those neurotransmitters, which can result in chaos in the brain. The balance and communication is off. The brain may develop a new narrative of protection and safety first as it attempts to make sense of the trauma experience, but this new narrative may not align with the concept of moving on and resuming the tasks of everyday life without stress, anxiety, and depression.

I quickly learned my traditional training in cognitive behavioral therapy was not wholly effective with individuals experiencing trauma reactions, since talk therapy could not reach the parts of the brain that were affected. In fact, many individuals who sought help from our team could not process the words used in traditional cognitive therapy models. They experienced such high levels of dysregulation in their bodies that until we engaged in activities that reregulated them, no amount of cognitive treatment could have a positive impact. If we simply offered a safe place to reframe their experiences and talk about their needs, they might have achieved temporary symptom relief. But addressing the whole body, and understanding the connection between it and the mind, was key to producing long-term relief. This is what appropriate trauma treatment looks like.

Temporary relief can be ineffective or, worse, damaging. We heard stories of individuals who became more dysregulated upon leaving a therapy session, as if a wound was reopened, and they did not have the tools or coping skills to self-soothe, so they adopted unhealthy means of relief, such as addictive behaviors, self-harming actions, isolation, depression, and anxiety.

THERAPEUTIC OPTIONS FOR TREATING TRAUMA

Reframing the maladaptive changes that an individual experiences in the aftermath of trauma may allow them greater insight and self-acceptance in lieu of feeling guilty or victimized. The goal is to identify these changes and shift the energy devoted to these hardening protective behaviors, transforming that energy into feelings of control, strength, and a newfound capacity for problem solving and decision making.

Because the field of trauma treatment is fast growing, it is helpful to spend time researching best practice treatments and their efficacy. However, we found that it was also extremely valuable to ask clients and treatment providers what they found most helpful or least effective. This information allowed us to recognize who we needed to engage with treatment that was not easily accessible.

These treatment modalities encompass fundamental techniques in grounding, mindfulness, relaxation, and breathing. Some modalities are creative, some more physical in nature, and a couple provide a means of articulating the traumatic experience through storytelling or acting out a similar scenario with an animal. Treatments we found to be most effective and widely used included the following:

- Acupuncture
- Aromatherapy
- Art Therapy
- Brainspotting
- Cognitive Behavioral Therapy
- Cognitive Processing Therapy
- Emotional Freedom Techniques/Tapping
- Eye Movement Desensitization and Reprocessing Therapy (EMDR)
- Equine- and Animal-Assisted Therapy
- Masgutova Neuro-Sensory Motor Reflex Integration (MNRI)
- Music Therapy
- Neurofeedback and Biofeedback
- Play Therapy
- Reiki
- Somatic Experiencing
- Transcranial Magnetic Stimulation (TMS)
- Trauma-Focused Cognitive Behavioral Therapy (TFCBT)
- Yoga

GRIEVING IS NORMAL FOLLOWING TRAUMA

Whether or not a traumatic event involves death, survivors must cope with loss. An individual that is grieving often works through the five commonly referenced stages of grief: denial, anger, bargaining, depression, and acceptance. The time it takes to move through these stages varies by individual, but we see this as a natural reaction to their loss. Thoughts, memories, and images of the deceased are prevalent. But with support, through time the emotional pain decreases and most people reenter the world with fulfillment and purpose.

COMPLICATED GRIEF

Complicated grief is a more intense, excessive form of anguish that occurs when trauma and grief coincide. The syndrome is commonly associated with the sudden loss of a loved one in an unpredictable manner that may be violent or traumatic in nature. When not addressed, risk factors set in and you develop long-term consequences—panic disorder, suicidal or homicidal ideation, terminated relationships, permanent attachment issues, avoidance of medical care, and chronic mental illness.

Complicated grief looks different than normal grief, depression, or anxiety. The symptoms are more intense and prolonged and manifest in a variety of challenging thoughts, feelings, and behaviors. Complicated grief is accompanied by a high level of distress that interferes with an individual's daily functioning. It can present as an excessive, all-consuming sadness that seems to deepen to the point of incessant negativity. Major depression, suicidal thoughts, and heightened anxiety often overlap with this syndrome.

Someone experiencing complicated grief may be consumed with guilt and ruminating over the circumstances of the death. They may express strong bitterness and anger. They likely will avoid spending time with family or friends, and while isolating, may try to get closer to the deceased by reviewing photos and keepsakes. They may try to recreate smells, sensations, and images that remind them of their loved one. They will describe a pervasive sense of emptiness.

PTSD can co-occur with complicated grief, but symptoms should be differentiated so that the response and treatment are specific to alleviate them both. PTSD is often rooted in fear and anxiety, while complicated grief is marked by overwhelming sadness and yearning for the person who passed. This may be expressed through statements like "Life will never be the same. We will never be the same. I can't stop remembering when my child was here with me."

Dealing with complicated grief is one of the most challenging aspects of community recovery work. The therapeutic trajectory is much longer and more intense than when helping someone recover from a more traditional or expected loss. For clinicians, the work can be exhausting and sometimes unsettling. In these cases, the typical stages of grief do not apply. Clinicians can feel like the client is not moving forward and question whether they are in fact making a positive impact. The reality is that individuals suffering from complicated grief require a higher level of endurance than the norm.

When you multiply this response by large numbers after a community tragedy, you begin to comprehend the magnitude of need for a specific, clinical, and supportive response. Disentangling complicated grief from the trauma response can feel, to recovery staff, like they are climbing a mountain under treacherous conditions with a heavy backpack that they want to drop. Yet they know the clues to the healing process are in that backpack and they have to stay with it until the storm passes.

IN SUMMARY

Community trauma and grief is both a collective and individual phenomenon that can complicate the healing process, so recovery efforts need to be delivered on both the group and individual level. It's also crucial for practitioners to have a clinical understanding of how the brain and body react in the wake of trauma. Being equipped to provide this awareness to those suffering gives them immeasurable relief and hope. Recovery is a process that starts with support and awareness and ends with a sense of resiliency. One transitions from feeling trapped in negative changes to their body and mind to feeling able to live in a positive, thoughtful, and present way.

Now that you have a better understanding of what might occur within your community, and who it may affect, how do you organize a broad scope of services? In Chapter Three, you'll learn how to set up your recovery team to provide the best service to your community.

CHAPTER THREE

THE TEAM APPROACH TO RECOVERY AND RESILIENCY

In order to prepare for a disaster, a community will need the physical as well as technological infrastructure to support recovery and access to experienced professionals who can deliver vital services. The coordination of these two factors requires a team approach.

Your team should fill specific staffing needs and expertise. The Department of Justice grant specified that our recovery and resiliency team should be hired to provide care coordination, trauma assessment and triage, and program development. I was the first one hired, and quickly worked to bring on the other professionals who would make up the NRRT team.

I am a psychotherapist with a background in clinical work, including trauma treatment and community mental health management. So I had the clinical and managerial experience to lead a recovery and resiliency team. But because of the profound nature of the trauma and complicated grief, when hiring my team I had to consider community dynamics, particularly the expectations of those most impacted.

One of my early meetings was with a small group of mothers whose children were killed in the shooting. They requested to meet with me before I had my team and infrastructure in place. I walked into the meeting naively assuming it would be an opportunity to introduce myself and present plans to provide continuing support. A few minutes into the meeting, one of the mothers leaned across the table and said, "Let's face it, you wouldn't have a job if my daughter wasn't murdered." While this interaction took me off guard, it was a useful introduction to the culture of the community and the nature of the work I would be immersed in for the next eighteen months. The magnitude of Newtown's pain was evident in her expression.

As I was introduced to residents and attended community forums, I heard distinct concerns about the team makeup and issues of trust. I mention this because healing professionals are typically used to being met with gratitude and trust. I learned quickly that in the shattered world of community loss, coping skills often manifest as a wall of skepticism if not outright resistance. Here are some concerns that came at me as I began to construct my team:

- Who are you, and how are you different from the hundreds of other people who promised help and fell short?
- I can't trust you; you haven't proven yourself.
- You will never know what it feels like to be in my shoes.

- You weren't here, so you can't understand what happened.

- I won't work with that care coordinator; it won't be confidential because her daughter attends the same school as mine.

- There is a member of your team who was involved in *that* organization after the shooting. Because she supported them in the past, we don't trust that she can be there for us now.

- You wouldn't have a job if my child were still alive.

- I got your letter in the mail and threw it in the garbage before opening it. I saw the label and figured it was just another group looking to exploit my grief.

These responses all came from well-intentioned people whose new normal is one of trauma and grief. A traumatized brain can operate from a place of fear and distrust. The fight-or-flight reaction is often still on hyper-alert, ready to engage. Because of this, I needed to hire staff that could manage these types of encounters knowing they came from true pain and suffering. My team needed to be prepared to accept resistance, fear, and anger. This is why there is no substitute for having a mix of staff with a clinical background and advanced trauma treatment skills in addition to familiarity with the community. Your staff needs the professional expertise to carry out their responsibilities, as well as a natural comfort connecting through painful and complicated emotional experiences. While the grant did not highlight this, I know the clinical experience of some of our team members was a key component to our success engaging, understanding, and developing an appropriate response at this early stage of the healing process.

I also quickly realized that my team would need a high tolerance for public scrutiny. Some community members were still so agitated by their experience, they couldn't accept our team's existence. All they saw was another person making empty promises. Their frame of reference was the many uninvited helpers and professionals who descended on Newtown making promises they did not deliver. Some had provided brief assistance, then disappeared without adequate follow-through. Others were simply unequipped to provide suitable treatment. There were, however, valued professionals who stayed the course and built a positive practice delivering quality services, and we needed to foster more of them. We needed to create a safe haven for the community, a place where staff emanated trust, nurturing, and clinical expertise.

This was my first introduction to the intense despair, confusion, fear, and uncertainty felt by those impacted by trauma. When you work in a community shaken to its core, the sense of trust and security it once enjoyed is now questioned and you will hear challenges to your decisions and judgment. Remember, Newtown was in the national spotlight for several months. The media presence was so pervasive that people felt exposed. For many, trust and security will be an issue forever. This translated to expectations that my team could not be trusted either. From their viewpoint, why trust us? They had also trusted that their children would go to school and come home that fateful day.

What's more, while team members need to have the right expertise to address relevant concerns, it is equally important to bring together staff that can blend their skills, collaborate with ease, and support each other. They need to work as a team: your group will not be productive or effective without supporting each other. As the team leader, I tried to promote a sense of connection within the team, and consequently we were able to leave work every day with some measure of emotional resiliency.

Encouraging self-care was also critical to minimizing vicarious trauma. When you work in a setting laden with emotion, especially one where individuals go to recount their pain, it is impossible not to absorb some of that trauma and feel the weight of their suffering. Grief work imparts a sense of helplessness to recovery practitioners because no matter how much relief you provide, you are never going to bring back the person who was lost. Trauma work is messy, too, as it's often accompanied by raw anger, fear, distrust, and decompensation. Answers are not simple, and relationships begin with baby steps to break down the wall of negative emotion.

RECOVERY TEAM ROLES

The team leader has many responsibilities. Perhaps the most important role outlined in the grant was to act as a liaison between the public and town leaders in the recovery process. This involved participating in collaborative meetings in which I would report challenges, share information, and negotiate compromises when community leaders were not on the same page. I also was tasked with setting up the infrastructure for the team's work—to provide perspective and a plan to address the recovery needs of individuals and groups affected by the tragedy. I put systems and policies in place to define the team's mission and scope of work, and spent the next eighteen months supporting that work while making decisions about our direction and efforts that would best serve this community.

I didn't know it before we started, but another responsibility my team would need to assume was the assessment of individuals and families for eligibility to receive local foundation and federal funds. These allocations had previously been managed by the state Office of Victim Services, but it was decided that the process should be managed locally instead of on the state level, so our team took on the role. This included setting up a documentation system to track the distributions. Financial management of the fund was taken over by the Newtown Sandy Hook Community Foundation, which also received and managed donations from other sources like the United Way and various private foundations. Not every team will require this, but it is likely that money will have a prominent role in the recovery work.

These are the recovery team positions that were spelled out in the grant:

- Community outreach liaison: My job was to hire the team, define the roles, assign tasks and responsibilities, develop the scope of recovery work including the mission and service plans, setup operations, provide ongoing supervision and oversight for recovery team efforts, provide communication and guidance to the community leaders for present and future recovery needs, and be accountable to state and federal organizations involved in the grant.
- Trauma specialist: this individual provided trauma-informed treatment, collaborated with content experts in the field of trauma recovery and grief work to develop initiatives, and formulated appropriate programming for

the community. The trauma specialist focused on building trusting relationships among the most impacted groups, including the individuals that witnessed the shooting, first responders, and other people in need of acute care. Newtown is a community of 27,000, but the grant provided for only one trauma specialist. We could have used one more person in this role. For my team, I acted as the second trauma specialist.

- Care coordinators: these resource specialists had backgrounds navigating mental health care. They held each client's hand and crafted individualized care plans to meet each person's unique needs. Care coordinators also assessed clients for reimbursement eligibility during intake interviews. Per our grant, I was able to hire two full-time care coordinators, but we needed coverage from three part-time employees instead.

- Project manager: a professional with an expertise in technology and accounting who was able to maintain operations, manage the team's online presence, and act as a liaison between insurance companies and mental health practitioners. On our team, this person was not only the initial contact for many who called the center, but also acted as the gatekeeper and claims processor for funds distributed by the Newtown Sandy Hook Community Foundation. After an assessment from a care coordinator, the project manager would collect and coordinate documentation to inform the Newtown Sandy Hook Community Foundation exactly who would receive funds.

FORMING AN EFFECTIVE RECOVERY TEAM

When I was ready to hire my team, I consulted town leaders regarding who was already providing community support. There were two separate camps that influenced my hiring decisions. One stated that it would only be comfortable with individuals who were from town and therefore already lived with the results of this tragedy. I imagined that competent local individuals working in the healing practice would be interested in continuing or sharing their work as a member of our team. But the second camp expressed a desire for professionals who had some distance from the event and were not impacted by the fracturing and other challenges that came with living close to the tragedy.

My trauma specialist was a licensed professional counselor with extensive credentials in the trauma care field. Although she was not a town resident, she had already established herself as a volunteer clinical leader with a memorial foundation and with families of children who were in the Sandy Hook School classrooms when the shooting occurred. She had earned their respect and was knowledgeable, thoughtful, and connected with other healers playing key roles in the community.

I had the funds to hire two full-time care coordinators, but decided to hire three part-time coordinators. Hiring three rather than two allowed for greater diversity in the background and expertise each coordinator brought to the role, as well as an increase in flexibility for coverage. If someone was on vacation or home with a sick child, I still had two coordinators in the office to handle appointments and walk-ins. When one of them was needed for an event, the other two could maintain access to care at the office. (Because of the nature of the work, we always avoided having one person manage the office traffic alone.)

The project manager's background was completely outside the scope of trauma. For this position, I was looking for someone able to build a website, assist in creating a data system for tracking insurance reimbursements for clients, and be the first point of contact for those seeking assistance. After interviewing several candidates, I went with someone who had warmth, positive energy, and a willingness to think outside the box to help build infrastructure there was no roadmap for. As mentioned earlier, the project manager also spent a large percentage of her time managing the financial resources available for individual recovery.

Skills Necessary for a Recovery Team

Each job required specific abilities. For our scope of work I made this skill list:

- Accounting

- Billing

- Communications/website/technology-based communication

- Database development and maintenance

- Interpersonal engagement

- Flexibility and creativity

- Healthy life balance and the ability to demonstrate self-care

- High-level clinical experience with trauma expertise

- Knowledge of best practices in treatments and programs

- Program development

- Public speaking

- Resilience (a thick skin)

- Resourcefulness

- Office management

BEST PRACTICES IN TEAM MANAGEMENT

Individuals do not always integrate naturally as a cohesive team. It may take some team-building exercises or rituals to nurture a sense of connectedness. We would go out for lunch on Fridays, plan holiday potlucks, make a point of celebrating birthdays, share family achievements or stressors, encourage each other professionally, and pair up for weekend job responsibilities. I held weekly meetings to discuss where we were as a staff in regards to our goals and programs. During these meetings, we discussed complicated cases for review while maintaining confidentiality. This was an opportunity to make sure everyone felt fully informed, and I invited everyone to add to the meeting agenda. I encouraged transparency and often took time to discuss individual challenges we each faced that related to the stressors of our work. We would also take a group walk during lunch breaks, or spontaneously sit together for a few minutes to share an experience. On occasion I would organize team wellness activities outside the office.

Even with these efforts, I faced a few challenges and sometimes had to navigate tense feelings among my team. I tend to operate with a transparent management style, addressing issues with an honest, direct approach. But because we were a small team in a small space, this approach did not always serve me well. Due to the layers of emotion that come with this work, vulnerabilities surfaced. And the longer the team worked together, the more opportunities there were for stress and exhaustion to affect the workplace dynamic.

Our team showed signs of this in our final months. I believe the combination of signing on to a job with lots of unknowns, and the knowledge that it was time limited, created an interesting dynamic as we winded down. You put your career on hold to participate in a project like this without knowing the personal impact it will have. Each team member had a different agenda moving forward. This would likely happen in other teams too. While one person might hope to continue doing healing work in the community in some capacity, another might be returning to a job they took a leave from. One team member might worry about securing a new job without a time gap, while another may be looking forward to taking time off to focus on family. When we worked together, there was a sense of cohesiveness and teamwork. As the project came to a close, there was some untangling of the team for individual futures. This mind-shift can promote stress, particularly under the circumstances of working in a traumatized community. This work is emotionally challenging. Though we were aware of the long-term needs of the community, after twenty-one months my team felt the heaviness of the work. As the project winds down you should pay close attention to how each member of your team manages self-care. This is a good time to de-stress together with connected activities.

Near the end of our eighteen-month grant, we were granted an extra three months to continue our work, further complicating our mood. Even if your team is in place for a defined period of time, it is helpful to remember that this timeline may shift. The extension allowed us to reach several more individuals for care coordination and carry out a few projects that we didn't think we had time to complete. However, emotionally we had to shift from focusing on an exit strategy and individual career steps to once again personally investing ourselves in more months of this challenging work. To some extent, it affected our energy and momentum.

As the team leader I kept an open-door policy and made it a point to hear and revisit accomplishments and challenges with each team member. I learned that each individual and group warranted a different approach to building rapport. This is not dissimilar to other clinical work, except that it comes with complicated cognitive challenges and emotional distress.

It is important that you always present as a team to the community. Collaboration is key. Most situations require many branches of assistance to complete the whole recovery package. But equally important—the staff needs each other for emotional support.

SETTING UP YOUR PHYSICAL SITE

When I was hired, it had already been decided by the board of directors that the project manager and myself would work in a shared space inside of a community foundation, and the care coordinators and trauma specialist would be in the basement of the police department. This decision was fraught with problems. First, I worried that if we had to send people to multiple locations to meet their needs, we would lose them in the process. Remember, these are individuals whose lives have been shattered, or turned upside down at best, and they may no longer feel capable of executing the simplest tasks.

I felt it was vitally important that the team work together in a single office space. I anticipated correctly that many individuals would enter our offices in need of multiple levels of assistance. It wasn't uncommon for someone to have an appointment with a care coordinator to discuss mental health resources and then need to sit with the project manager to review the financial assistance options. It was also common for people to walk in the door not knowing what services they needed and, after explaining their concerns to a care coordinator, find themselves in a state of crisis. We would then walk them across the hall for an impromptu meeting with the trauma specialist.

On one occasion, a mother who had lost a child in the shooting came in with an armful of medical and mental health insurance statements, asking, "Can you help me make sense of these?" A care coordinator spread them out on a table, organized, and sorted them. The project manager then made calls to the insurance company and service providers. The woman left with a sense of relief at having resolved the issue.

But one of the most important reasons to place your team together is to promote a sense of camaraderie and community, and to encourage group- and self-care. I'll say it again: this work is emotionally taxing. There are times when a team member feels stuck, but another member has the resource he or she needs. At times, team members need to talk about the impact this work is having on them and their families. And there are certainly opportunities for team members to share positive distractions—the happy moments in life, like a new litter of puppies, a child being accepted to college, or an engagement announcement.

Aside from this concern, I believed housing even part of our office in a police station could trigger the very trauma symptoms we were hired to alleviate. It was hard enough for some residents to hear police sirens on the streets and not fall into flashbacks. This type of public venue would not provide the privacy and confidentiality we needed, either. Confidentiality is key to team success, and at the same time it is a hurdle. I mentioned the concerns that some expressed about who made up our team. "Are they outsiders or insiders?" was the question. In a small community this can be an issue; in a larger city, it may not. Regardless, most individuals crossing your path will feel vulnerable and perhaps exposed. Summoning the courage to walk in the door might have taken days or weeks. They may be thinking, "I shouldn't get this help. Others are more in need than me." Or they may have no idea what is wrong other than to say, "I cannot seem to get my life together." While everyone can benefit from hearing that they are not alone and that their current state is understandable, everyone wants to know they are protected and their vulnerability will not be further exposed.

Confidentiality is sacred in this work. Without it your site could be very quiet, not to mention the liability concerns. Make sure you set up your workplace with the highest professional ethics standards and that your team understands, unequivocally, that what happens at the center stays at the center. Meeting people where they are at, building trust, and establishing a level of competency that is flexible, comprehensive care driven, and trauma informed is vital to your success. Doing this with high ethical standards will ensure respect and a flow of referrals. Falling down in this area means instant failure, and it takes a long time to build trust back.

I pushed back on the original location and pounded the pavement to locate a space that fit my criteria and budget. I wanted a space that offered a sense of welcoming, relaxed comfort, as well as privacy for confidential meetings. In the clinical realm this is often referred to as "trauma informed." In the end, the first selectwoman, head of the Newtown government, found the perfect spot in an old home situated amidst several municipal buildings, on a campus that once housed a mental institution. The space was close to public buildings but stood alone, had separate parking, and included plenty of outdoor space to walk with a client or get fresh air. It was easy to find and offered that much-needed sense of privacy. We took great efforts to advertise the location and phone number for walk-ins and appointments. The phone had a back-up line to prevent anyone from receiving a busy signal.

DEFINING AND INTRODUCING THE TEAM TO THE COMMUNITY

Once the team was hired, I worked to establish our role and communicate this mission to the community. While it is important to employ your staff and get to work on the community recovery, getting a feel for the dynamics and expectations of the community first can be helpful. Because I was coming to the work eighteen months after the tragedy, I had to acknowledge that there had already been some lessons learned and assumptions made based on successful and unsuccessful attempts to address the community's needs through recovery programming. While you don't want your decisions colored by too many opinions, you can minimize stress by first gaining an understanding of what has worked and who is trusted.

Thankfully, a community assessment report had been completed previously by a local psychologist, Dr. Jill Baron. It evolved from interviews and discussions with community members and leaders. This document was informative and gave me an idea of where to focus the team's efforts. We would provide a combination of very intimate and intensive individual assistance, and small- and large-scale programming for support, education, and training.

Every team's approach to community recovery and resiliency will evolve through time, and as I've stated it is important to remain flexible, as your roles and scope will change. The areas of focus I chose were:

- Developing a single, direct access site
- Providing care coordination
- Offering trauma treatment
- Assessing for financial reimbursement
- Creating education and support programs for the entire Newtown community

ADVERTISING OUR SERVICES

Getting the word out and establishing a presence is as important as setting up a welcoming center. People won't walk in the door if they don't know who you are, understand how to find you, or have awareness of the value you provide. We often attended community events such as Earth Day festivals, school open houses, foundation events, and memorials. We created wellness events that targeted specific groups and built awareness of our work. We set up meetings to address school counselors, parent-teacher associations, pediatricians, primary care physicians, nonprofit organizations, and religious groups.

Every member of the team had a business card. We developed glossy marketing materials that we left at places like the town hall, library, grocery stores, schools, and the public gym. The brochures highlighted core components of our work, our contact information, and the website. We developed a simple logo to use in all written correspondence, as well as event notifications and our center sign.

We invited the local newspaper to photograph the team and our office, and asked them back several times throughout our tenure to review our work and promote new events. Invitations went out in several formats: mail, email, town publications, and on our website. We attended every school's open house and addressed parents. We met with school social workers to remind them of our presence and establish a collaborative relationship.

The following text was used to define The Newtown Recovery and Resiliency Team:

The Recovery and Resiliency Team

- We are a skilled six-person team of licensed professionals and educators
- Our goal is to bring the community together to collaborate on many levels
- We offer direction and support to those impacted by the Sandy Hook tragedy

Our Mission

The Recovery and Resiliency Team was created to provide resources and facilitate communication between service providers and funding sources, while assisting in the ongoing assessment of the community's present and future needs.

Our Role in the Community

We offer direction and support to those impacted by the Sandy Hook tragedy.

Services include:

- Centralized access to mental health resources
- Enhancing communication between helping professionals

- Problem-solving support to address ongoing needs
- Assistance in determining eligibility for, and connecting to, funding sources
- Filling in gaps of recovery services
- Providing support to individuals and families, our schools, emergency responders, and the community at-large
- Programming to foster resiliency

PARTNERING THE TEAM WITH THE COMMUNITY

Once the team was in place, the next step was to meet with key service providers in town to better understand where we should focus our efforts. The entire team set out to form bridges between these partners. This occurred in a number of ways: setting up meet-and-greets with school professionals, attending community events sponsored by other organizations or municipal departments, accepting invitations to speak at informational or planning meetings, connecting with organizations acknowledged in the DOJ grant to support their work, offering to promote the work of others on our website, asking questions about what others were doing and how we could assist, and addressing recovery needs of groups that asked for help. One of the few things we knew from the get-go was that while we needed to be available for individual support, we had to develop community programming in collaboration with existing partners too. Initially we focused on building those relationships, fostering trust, and creating a positive, respectful presence.

With mass tragedy, there is often a great deal of fracturing, and I knew it was important to avoid contributing to this phenomenon.

Presenting as the "resident experts" who had come to fix the community would not have been well received. This was especially true in Newtown, where in the previous eighteen months a flood of other providers had, with some exceptions, caused more pervasive problems.

Engaging with individuals and each impacted group was probably the most important aspect of our agenda, and *how* we engaged each group was unique. As stated before, the way we needed to approach first responders differed greatly from the way we engaged with families who had lost a child. Sometimes recovery and resiliency work is a practice in absorbing the pain that comes at you, since there is nothing you can say or do to take away that pain. Often, you simply need to hold space with an impacted individual. This means not leading with your own agenda; you match where the person is at, allowing them to just *be* while you provide a sense of safety and nurturing until they are ready to change. Never underestimate the healing power of this kind of acceptance, though you may go home at the end of the day feeling bruised and battered yourself.

When at the table with another organization or town department that expresses a strong desire for certain types of services or programming, it's important to jump on board and say, "How can we help?" With this attitude, you will find that when you are in need of resources or funds, the organizations you've partnered with will be more inclined to help. We presented the message that the NRRT was available to form collaborative partnerships that would ensure success. Those groups and organizations that embraced this type of collaboration became our strongest supporters.

I also learned that I could not always change my style of working or pretend to be an expert with all groups. It was important to bring in experts who could establish respect and acceptance with impacted groups. Sometimes they were survivors who understood a language and culture that I did not, such as retired police officers who had responded to 9/11 to work with our cops, teachers who had lived through school shootings, or a man who had lost his child and built a career assisting other parents with grief. This can allow for breakthroughs. I will provide more detail on this later in the book, but understand that you will not have all the answers and cannot possibly command instantaneous clout with every group. When you encounter pushback on your ideas or responses, it may be because the people receiving your message are not ready to hear it from you. But they may be willing to listen to someone who has already proven him or herself and is immersed in their language and culture.

Some of the professionals I found important to partner with were:

- The town's public health, human resources, finance, social services, and recreational department directors
- The school district's superintendent, principals, counselors, and PTA presidents
- The police chief, police union representatives, and police communications director
- Fire and EMT departments
- Trauma treatment providers who were present during the crisis management phase
- Clinical professionals who provided guidance and workshops before our team

- Substance abuse prevention and support organizations
- Local clergy
- Pediatricians and primary care providers
- Local foundations, youth organizations, creative arts centers, senior centers, and gyms
- Documentarians who had been vetted
- Coordinators for other grants

WHAT WE ACCOMPLISHED

In a total of twenty-one months my team provided support to nearly 900 individuals on a care-coordination level and engaged countless more community members through training, education, and outreach. We created a calendar of community events and programs. We focused on building relationships, fostering trust, and creating a positive, respectful presence. We became part of the town fabric.

Don't underestimate the amount of time and energy this can take. Often it feels like you took one step forward and two steps back. The progress that takes place in a community recovery office is hard to measure. Sometimes a client walks away and you know you had a positive impact. Other times a client leaves and you question whether you were helpful at all. Your efforts may seem to be effective for some, but appear to evoke pain or lack an effect for others. A program might have been presented at a perfect time for some, but others may not feel capable of absorbing that information yet. You may win a fight to acknowledge that a certain group has needs to address, only to find out that you have to raise the money to service those issues. You might successfully expose an area of weakness that has prevented true healing, but lack authority to correct the problem. You might help hundreds, knowing that's just the tip of the iceberg. On a day that you receive a thank-you card for your valuable work, another note questions your efforts. You may feel great about sharing your experience with others as they venture into this field, only to be criticized for fear that your narrative will expose people. You may say no to funding requests from impacted people because new criteria have been set to preserve that money, to which the individuals express disappointment.

What I learned was that:

- Holding space for grief, walking beside someone during a time of need, creating a safe space without judgment, and regulating symptoms of trauma is extremely valuable.
- No program can be "one and done." Programs and treatment must be repeated to reach each individual effectively. Create permanent outlines and materials for each recovery team.
- If someone cannot hear your message, they will find their way back when ready.
- Sometimes the bigger issues require you to delegate and stay behind the scenes. This may mean you never get the credit but can still feel good about the results.
- Never take adverse responses personally. The community you are servicing is reacting with fear and pain.
- Do not underestimate the power of helping one person. They will go out in the community and help others.

IN SUMMARY

The best approach to the recovery of a community is as a team. I cannot imagine taking this task on as a sole practitioner, even if the community was smaller in size and scope. One person cannot possibly have the expertise or emotional endurance to cover it all.

Although you may not have an abundance of time, thoughtfully plan and evaluate every part of the process to ensure success. Choosing the right staff, location, priorities, communication strategies, mission, and policies is as important as the actual recovery work. While there is always room for reevaluation and flexibility, starting off confident that you have the right people and practices is vital. When interacting with traumatized individuals who can come in feeling broken and lost, making the right impression with a trauma-focused approach is important. It may be difficult to correct this later because many are already feeling exposed and distrustful. Finally, pay close attention to your and your staff's own wellness. That can be the difference between feeling vulnerable, wounded, and unable to continue the work, and feeling healthy, positive, and resilient.

CHAPTER FOUR

COMPREHENSIVE CARE COORDINATION

C are coordination is defined as a "client-centered, accessible approach to meeting the therapeutic needs of an individual." From a mental health perspective, this model looks to create an all-inclusive therapeutic plan to address a client's psychosocial, medical, and financial needs. The plan should be personalized to bolster the client's strengths and address weaknesses, including the unique circumstances or vulnerabilities that bring the client into the office.

Comprehensive care coordination should feel like a support system for individuals, families, and groups that combines assessment, resources, crisis management, and treatment. It's like hiring an insurance representative to handle all your needs and claims with a mindful approach to address trauma and wellness. The client builds a relationship with the care coordinator and relies on that representative to be there and make sure each need is addressed successfully. The care coordination model should increase the effectiveness of connection because it reduces potential obstacles to securing treatment and assistance. The result is better outcomes and higher rates of symptom reduction. I believe every town should have a dedicated service to help coordinate or navigate care when disaster strikes.

Care coordination was the core service the NRRT provided, and was fundamental to assessing each individual who walked through our doors. Having a professional readily available to understand the complexities of trauma, develop a plan, and organize its components is what comprehensive care coordination is all about. As I have mentioned, when an individual experiences the impact of trauma, they often lack words to express their needs or the capability to define the magnitude of change and dysfunction they feel. At times an entire subgroup of the community may express similar concerns, indicating an entire system is cracking. When this information is collected uniformly, the needs of these groups can be reported and evaluated for a plan of action. In these cases, there is no substitute for comprehensive care coordination. It should be trauma informed and clinically sound, and the coordinators should be experts in recovery and resiliency.

The most effective type of care coordination for our community was a melding of classic social work with a clinical approach to address the medical and emotional needs of each individual. A care coordinator should be well versed in resources that address basic needs as well as complex and diverse issues, since a multi-layered plan is often necessary. For example, we found that people with mental health issues can also benefit from health and wellness resources or non-traditional therapeutic modalities.

Our experience taught us that care coordination had to begin the minute someone expressed a need for assistance, and could only end successfully with ongoing follow-up. A treatment plan was always established during the initial assessment intake.

Once my care coordinators identified which services would be most effective, we not only connected the patient to those services, but also contacted his or her existing health care providers, school supports, family supports, etc., so that everyone was looped in. The care coordinators were not simply handing out names and numbers. They made the phone calls, set up the appointments, secured the funds, called the insurance company, and arranged an immediate support network if warranted. In the end, each individual had a tailored program that was well monitored.

The plan for treatment should be documented and given to the individual for personal follow-through with clearly spelled-out contacts for immediate assistance. We followed up through direct phone calls to the clients, set up new appointments for within a week or less, and asked if they would like a check-in call in a few days. If the plan needed to be tweaked, we wanted to catch that sooner rather than later.

Prior to Implementing a Care Coordination Model:

1. Build relationships with community organizations, treatment providers, and other entities that have already provided assistance. This involves engaging on many levels to establish professionalism, respect, awareness, and trust

2. Begin to assess the immediate and ongoing needs of people impacted by the tragedy

3. Formulate a team of care coordinators. A staff of varied backgrounds and expertise is recommended

4. Educate and prepare staff to provide immediate stabilization

5. Be prepared with appropriate, vetted therapy and wellness resources

SETTING UP A CARE COORDINATION OFFICE

Each community will need care coordination professionals who match with the nature of the tragedy and presenting issues. For example, culturally diverse or bilingual coordinators may be needed. Circumstances may necessitate coordinators who are well versed in physical injury or environmental hazards. There may be a need for gender-specific coordinators, those trained in developmental issues, or coordinators who have a background in human resources, disability claims, or legal expertise.

The model we created involved the development of a unique relationship between a single, trauma-informed care coordinator and an individual client. The matching often started with our trauma specialist, who acted as the supervisor to the care coordinators. She would screen each potential client and assign them to a care coordinator. By pre-screening the cases, the trauma specialist became aware of each client's personal situation.

I employed three care coordinators of different backgrounds and areas of expertise in order to fulfill the town's initial assessed needs. Two coordinators had already been working in Newtown in the same capacity under a small grant from the American Pediatric Association, and their contracts were about to end. One was a Sandy Hook resident and licensed clinical social worker whose daughter was in the school on the day of the shooting. The second was a registered nurse whose career history included community work assisting children and families with special health care needs. These individuals had already built a resource bank and proven themselves as professionals committed to assisting many families. The third individual was a Newtown resident with a background in communications and parenting education. She brought to the table many valuable connections she had made through work at a grassroots organization developed to address the personal and political issues the tragedy had revealed. Together, the resources these three coordinators brought and the system they built to address the families' needs provided a tremendous foundation for the entire team. They each worked part-time and kept hours that varied, covering early mornings and evenings to accommodate our clients' schedules. The coordinators were flexible and open to holding phone or in-person meetings on weekends or outside their regular work hours. This way, we had direct site access and central phone line coverage five days a week. Each care coordinator had a voicemail system too, so clients could leave confidential messages.

All the coordinators worked in our office. Because of space constraints, they worked together in one large room located at the center's entrance so anyone walking in would be immediately greeted by a care coordinator. Each had her own desk and phone situated on the periphery of the room; in the center was a conference table and chairs. The room also had file cabinets, a copy machine, bookshelves for resource material, and a whiteboard displaying the most recent resource and provider information. The layout meant that when an individual session was scheduled, the other coordinators either had to leave the room or the coordinator conducting the meeting needed to reserve another space. As I reflect back on this set-up, I believe it was invaluable for the coordinators to be together freely sharing their thoughts, experiences, collective skills, and resources. Having more than one professional wrap their head around a case was often very helpful.

When not working with an individual, care coordinators visited providers to arrange for them to present their services to the community. This was our way of vetting professionals. And I believe we succeeded in matching clients to providers and programs without too much trial and error because the care coordinators spent a great deal of time getting to know the providers. We knew what differentiated one provider from another. We knew which insurances they accepted, what their hours were, if they had openings, and what age range they felt most comfortable treating. If there were red flags about a provider, we were aware and could steer someone in a different direction.

Our care coordinators kept a whiteboard listing providers and their availability—information that could change daily. While the care coordinators checked in with providers, others would call in to report that they had openings. When new providers contacted us, we invited them into our office to discuss their services with the entire team.

Fostering relationships with providers increased our credibility with clients, and that collaborative spirit ensured a greater level of success because clients' needs were met with appropriate resources.

Care coordinators are the front end of the recovery operation. Often the first line of assistance, they immerse themselves in the lives of the impacted individuals. You want your coordinators focused on the client, providing that boots-on-the-ground service. But since their job is emotionally difficult, try to shield them from concerns they may have no control over. You also want them to recognize that they are aiding community recovery in a big way. This is a tricky line to draw. I had regular team meetings, which involved all staff, as well as meetings with only care coordinators, to address their specific concerns. Protecting your team from negativity that may come about will help maintain their emotional balance and prevent burnout.

THE FINANCIAL SIDE OF CARE COORDINATION

Then there was the financial element: determining which treatment options a client's insurance would cover and the funding availability to cover any gaps. In later chapters I will explain in detail how we matched funds from our block grant, private donors, and social services to compensate for inadequate health insurance coverage when necessary. This work took countless hours of collaboration and a systematic approach with guidelines for eligibility and reimbursable services. However, before getting to this step, care coordinators, as part of the assessment, determined each individual's financial need as it related to their plan for appropriate services. It would not have been helpful to recommended services the individual could not afford or attain through some other resource.

ASSESSING ROUTINE VERSUS URGENT/ACUTE CLINICAL NEEDS

There is no common profile for an individual experiencing a trauma reaction. We quickly learned that each person's experience and life changes were unique. The factors that contribute to this phenomenon are: proximity to the tragic event, a sense of responsibility concerning the event, emotional healthiness prior to the event, presence or lack of supports before and after the event, past trauma history, stress and a capacity to cope with stress prior to the event, length of time before seeking assistance, perceived sense of purpose in life, and sense of trust or safety. The care coordinator had privacy releases signed so she could speak with an emergency contact, spouse, and/or provider if need be.

Asking clinical and psychosocial questions is a vital part of the assessment; it allows the care coordinator to determine where a person is at and whether their needs are acute. For instance, high-risk behavior like heavy drinking is the only thing John can use to cope with the disruptive, horrific script on continuous replay in his mind. John may be someone who abused alcohol in the past, "but only on weekends when I didn't have to go to work." John now drinks every morning to get through the day and stops in a park on his way home to drink a little more before facing his family in the evening. He makes mistakes on the job and is developing an "I just don't care" attitude. If not addressed in an acute way, you can see how quickly John's personal life may soon crumble around him—family relationships start to deteriorate, job security is jeopardized, health risks ensue, safety risks increase for John and those in his support circle, and clinical depression sets in. While John is not expressing that he is at immediate or imminent risk, this is a case that a care coordinator will arrange services for immediately, to prevent John from losing the momentum to get help.

Jane seeks assistance because she cannot go to bed at night without recounting the name of every victim who didn't survive the shooting. "I'm functioning but I can't relax," she says. "I can't enjoy life—it doesn't seem fair. Nothing is enjoyable anymore, actually, but I still get up every day for my family and my community." In this case, the care coordinator will likely ask for greater detail on the rituals or changes that have caused exhaustion and emotional overload. There may be education needed about trauma's effect on the brain. They would discuss any past participation in healthy, adrenaline-based activities and whether those can be resurrected even though Jane feels like she has no energy for such activities. The coordinator would also explore options for a cognitive therapist, as well as healthy therapies such as yoga or aromatherapy.

Julie, a high school social worker, refers Kyle because he is clearly unfocused, missing a lot of class, and acting belligerent. The school or parent may call for the appointment. Depending on the child's age or level of resistance, an assigned care coordinator may request that the parent bring the child in, or meet alone with the parent. If the child comes in, the coordinator may have time alone with them. The assessment involves gathering his behavioral history before and after the tragic event. Often you find out not only the child's connection, but the family's as well. Kyle was a camp counselor who had one of the non-surviving children in his camp section. Kyle's mother may now be spending several nights a week at foundation meetings to contribute to a cause that has grown out of the tragedy. When questioned, Kyle demonstrates a confusion and anger that seem to stick with him throughout each day. The care coordinator can, with the parent's permission, explore preferences to match him with a therapist and set up their first appointment. The care coordinator offers insight and guidance to Kyle and his parent, and arranges for a follow-up appointment at the center.

David sat on the school bus every morning next to a friend who was killed in the shooting. He is unable to find pleasure now in daily activities and is often afraid to go to school. Kate's sibling was trapped at the scene, feeling helpless as she waited in lockdown. Tina feels like it is pointless to work hard to get into college when life can be dashed away in minutes. In cases like these, the care coordinator may want to meet a few times with the family and/or child to build trust and gain positive momentum as a plan with their direct input is put in place.

It's very important that a care coordinator educate the parent on why and how these changes may have resulted from secondary trauma. It's ultra-important, too, that the coordinator ask about the parent's own support system and outlets for healthy balance. The coordinator should then formulate a plan for treatment that includes the child's interests as well as clinical presentation. If the child has difficulty expressing himself verbally, art therapy may be suggested. If the child loves music, music therapy may be a good match. And if the child gravitates towards animals or has a nurturing quality, equine therapy may be of great help. The coordinator should also suggest resources for the parent and other affected family members. If a parent expresses concern about financial stress because many of these treatments are not covered through insurance, the coordinator might send the parent to the project manager or a designated team member in charge of funding resources to discuss options. The care coordinator might also take the time to reach out to a foundation or organization that has committed funds for community treatment. Because this plan may take a few meetings to develop, when it is ready the coordinator can offer a follow-up meeting or phone call to assure success accessing these resources.

THE IMPORTANCE OF COLLECTING DATA

It is crucial to begin the recovery team process knowing what information will be important to collect for current and future reports. This involved developing a record of specific information and a system to house and extract it. Because I was not given any guidelines in this area, I began with thoughtful assumptions of what might be interesting and important to capture, but several months into our work I realized there were gaps. This made for very labor-intensive data extraction later in the game. For instance, we did not capture any baseline information, which may have been helpful in dictating future needs. Comparing the layers of assistance and timeframes for recovery to past supports, socioeconomics, past traumas, or psychiatric history could have been informative. As we were winding down, it was decided that we should try to capture the numbers of reoccurrences, or visits to the center for new issues, in an attempt to inform future town planning needs. This was not initially reported on the needs assessment form, so we had to go back through each paper file and count reoccurrences.

Several months into our work, I developed a new document to tally presenting problems. When we started looking at the numbers for specific presenting problems, we could create reports that suggested areas to focus on for future programming, including areas the town may have wanted to continue funding and thoughts on the tragedy's impact and trajectory.

You can capture this type of baseline information early in your work, and continually look at trends and trajectories of what treatments and therapies are effective, how many times an individual seeks assistance, and what needs to prioritize in each of these situations. Routinely looking at this data also helped me educate town leaders on what we had seen and why we put effort into a certain program or area of need.

Each tragedy will have specific data collection needs. For example, if there was a shooting in a high school, such as the incident in Parkland, Florida, a large number of parents might be concerned that their children's grades have dropped since the tragedy. This may spark a conversation between you and the school's superintendent, who can then address the concern with parents directly. Effects on school performance were a concern for some parents and educators in Newtown. When I mentioned their worries to the school principal and superintendent, I was shown research that in fact did not support this premise. It was helpful to be able to deliver this message to concerned parents.

We started with the checklist listed below, recording what each individual came in for assistance with. The care coordinator would document the expressed concerns and her assessed concerns. For instance, an individual might report trouble sleeping and self-medicating with alcohol. The care coordinator might determine through the assessment process that their work-life was also affected, since the individual had less ability to work overtime, which caused financial and marital stress.

To do this, care coordinators should be trained to ask historical questions. For instance, if someone reports struggling in a relationship, ask if this was an issue before the tragedy. Had they attended couples counseling in the past? Were there abusive patterns or other troubling behaviors before? If a child needs treatment for depression or exhibits at-risk behaviors like self-mutilation, it would be important to capture any prior history of such behaviors and/or treatment. If an individual asks for funds for a gym membership or yoga instruction because she believes it will improve her health and wellness, it might be useful to record how many people are adding this activity to their routines because they find it beneficial. Or are you mostly seeing those who embraced health and fitness before the tragedy turning to it for ongoing support?

Your psychosocial assessment may include some simple questions to discern whether a specific need is related to the tragedy. It might also be beneficial to allow space to record any narrative details that further explain the dynamics of the situation. Knowing ahead of time how you will use the information is helpful. Might it be important to know how many times an individual has reached out for help? Would multiple occurrences of the use of your services be considered positive or negative? How will you determine if a concern or issue has been triggered by exposure to the tragedy or stressors associated with the tragedy? For example, imagine an individual comes into your office asking for assistance to secure and fund substance abuse treatment. You find out that this person had been in treatment prior to the tragedy. But now that you are aware that it was a preexisting condition, will that matter when asking for funds? Do you look at this latest occurrence as an exacerbation of symptoms because of the tragedy?

Another example is that of a parent who asks for summer basketball camp funds for a child who lost a sibling in the shooting, because they feel it might be emotionally beneficial. You learn that the child attended the camp in the past. For data collection purposes you have to think: Is this a financial hardship because the family has dealt with financial stressors since the death of a child? Does it matter if the outcome is beneficial?

However, even if you do not have a complete picture of how your data may be utilized in the end, it is still important to collect as much as you can from the beginning. Because we didn't anticipate the magnitude of Newtown's long-term needs in the beginning, we had to go back and interpret our files from the initial few months to capture some of this information and gain a clearer picture. The data was there, but it needed to be extracted.

THE CARE COORDINATION PROCESS

1. **Telephone connection from referral sources:** Referrals for care coordination can be made from the individual themselves, a family member, friend, or an outside source such as a physician or school personnel. If you have a visible presence in the community, you will likely get referrals for someone in crisis. The school may send a child or parent to you; a supervisor might send their staff to you; a friend may drive someone over to see you; a police officer might call to say they are bringing someone over; the town social service department may request that an individual contact you; the local pharmacist might hand someone your card and strongly advise that they get a ride over. Gathering basic information on the phone from a referral can help match the individual to a coordinator, who may then prepare for the individual's arrival.

2. **Face-to-face assessment of an impacted individual:** The following questions should be included in the assessment process:

   - What is the presenting problem/reason the client is seeking help?
   - What symptoms are the client currently experiencing?
   - What is their association to the tragedy?
   - What are the client's strengths and weaknesses?
   - Is there a safety issue? Is the client at risk? Is the risk imminent? Is there potential for self-harm or for others to be harmed?
   - What are the client's existing psychosocial supports?
   - What limitations and/or challenges are the client experiencing

that pose a barrier to accessing the supports they need? For instance, the fear of losing their job if issues are exposed, or the inability to maintain family responsibilities while working through the healing process.

- Do you have consent for communication with collateral supports?
- What are the funding needs?
- What is the client's availability for appointments?
- What is the client's insurance coverage and policy number?
- Does the client have a gender preference for a therapist or treatment provider?
- What geographic location is the client willing to travel to? Are there transportation challenges?

3. Research that takes place following the assessment:

- Insurance network: phone calls to the company about benefits and procedures
- Assessment of immediacy or urgency. Do the needs and concerns imply that an individual or family is at risk of immediate decompensation or without basic needs such as food and housing?
- Clinically suggested best practice treatments for presenting problem
- Specific gender requests or concerns (due to trauma history, etc.)
- Availability of client
- Barriers to successful follow-through
- Outside funding sources, if applicable

After the initial assessment, follow-up calls and appointments are made by the care coordinator. These should be documented so other team members have access to the plan in the absence of the care coordinator. The client also has their care coordinator's phone number and the understanding that they can reach out between appointments if assistance is needed. Privacy releases are signed and the care coordinator has contact information for the client's providers and emergency supports.

DOCUMENTATION AND CONFIDENTIALITY

We chose to keep a paper chart on each client, but if there is sufficient funding, an electronic record may be ideal. We kept an electronic database for reporting and funding purposes, and the project manager managed the system. I did not want multiple individuals entering information into that database. I was concerned about errors and inconsistencies and, for confidentiality purposes, did not want personal or clinical information housed in a widely-accessed electronic system.

To avoid bogging the care coordination process down with excessive paperwork, coordinators kept a separate chart on each client that contained assessment information, notes, and streamlined forms. If an individual showed up or called seeking immediate assistance and their coordinator was not available, the individual's history and notes were still there.

SAMPLE FORMS

We created a series of forms that can be adapted to your community's particular needs.

1. Initial Assessment: This form was duplicated and passed on to the project manager so she could enter basic clinical and demographic data into her database for future reporting.

INITIAL REQUEST FOR ASSISTANCE

Care Coordinator: _____   Family ID: _____

Request Date: _____

Applicant Information

First Name   _MI_   _Last Name_

Address   _City_   _State_   _Zip_

Home telephone number   _Cell phone number_   _E-mail address_

Date of Birth   _If under the age of 18, Parent/Guardian Name_

Collateral Sources

Do you have health insurance?   ❑ Yes   ❑ No

If yes, please answer the following questions:

Health insurance carrier: _____

Check one: ❑ Individual   ❑ Family

Deductible: _____ **% After Deductible is Met:** _____

Copay(s): _____

Do you have out-of-network benefits? ❑ Yes   ❑ No

Would you like us to contact your insurance company

to inquire about your benefits?   ❑ Yes   ❑ No

If yes, please sign our permission to contact form (will be sent via email)

Demographics

Gender: ❑ Male   ❑ Female   ❑ Transgender   ❑ Unknown

Age: ❑ 0–10 ❑ 11–17 ❑ 18–30 ❑ 31–44 ❑ 45–64 ❑ 65+ ❑ Unknown

INITIAL REQUEST FOR ASSISTANCE (CONT.)

Race: ❑ White   ❑ Black or African American

❑ American Indian and Alaska Native   ❑ Asian

❑ Native Hawaiian and   ❑ Some Other Race

Other Pacific Islander   ❑ Unknown

Disability Status: ❑ People with Disabilities   ❑ No/Unknown Disabilities

Please check all that apply:

❑ Parent of a Victim of Homicide   ❑ Family Member of Homicide Victim

❑ SHES Survivor/Witness   ❑ SHES Survivor/Witness Parent

❑ SHES Survivor/Witness Family Member   ❑ SHES Student

❑ SHES Parent   ❑ SHES Family Member

❑ SHES Teacher   ❑ SHES Personnel/Staff

❑ Student of Another Newtown School   ❑ Parent—Other Newtown School

❑ Teacher—Other Newtown School   ❑ Newtown Resident

❑ Personnel/Staff of Another Newtown school

❑ First Responder *(police, fire, emergency personnel)*

❑ First Responder Family Member

❑ Individuals Indirectly Connected to the Incident: _____

❑ Other: _____

Services Requested:
(Please check all that apply)

❑ Mental Health   ❑ Prescription(s)

❑ Health & Wellness   ❑ Acupuncture/Chiropractic Care

❑ Equine-Assisted Therapy (EAT)   ❑ Massage

❑ Physical Health and Fitness Activities   ❑ Other Alternative: _____

❑ Social/Emotional Support and Enrichment Activities for Children

2. Form to capture initial reasons for assistance:

REASONS FOR SEEKING SUPPORT FROM NRRT

*(For all that apply, place a **P** for primary and **S** for secondary. Check your initials)*

_____ Abuse	_____ Neurological issues
_____ Addiction-alcohol	_____ Parenting
_____ Addiction-substances	_____ Personality issues
_____ Addiction-sex	_____ Pregnancy related
_____ Addiction-gambling	_____ Psychological assessment
_____ Anger	_____ Psychotherapy
_____ Anxiety	_____ Relationship ossues
_____ Aging	_____ School related anxiety
_____ Basic needs	_____ Self harming behaviors
_____ Behavioral problems	_____ Sexual issues (non-addiction)
_____ Career concerns	_____ Sleep problems
_____ Chronic pain	_____ Smoking
_____ Child abuse/neglect	_____ Social difficulties
_____ Depression	_____ Stress
_____ Divorce	_____ Suicidal ideation
_____ Domestic violence/ partner abuse/neglect	_____ Truancy
_____ Education	_____ Tutoring
_____ Eating disorder	_____ Weight gain
_____ Financial stress	_____ Work issues
_____ Grief and loss	_____ Holiday/anniversary coping
_____ Health insurance	_____ Medication

3. Form for Case Notes:

CASE NOTES

Name:_____ DOB: _____

Date: _____ Care Coordinator: _____

Address: _____ Phone Number: _____

_____ Insurance Carrier: _____

═══════════════ **Applicant Request:** ═══════════════

_____
_____
_____

═══════ **Care Coordinator Needs Assessment:** ═══════

_____
_____
_____
_____
_____
_____
_____
_____

═══════════ **Follow-Up Recommendations:** ═══════════

_____
_____
_____

Next Meeting Date: _____   ❑ N/A

Care Coordinator Signature: _____

4. Progress Form:

PROGRESS NOTES

Name:_____ DOB: _____

_____

_____

_____

_____

_____

_____

_____

Care Coordinator Signature: _____ **Date:** _____

_____

_____

_____

_____

_____

_____

Care Coordinator Signature: _____ **Date:** _____

_____

_____

_____

_____

_____

_____

Care Coordinator Signature: _____ **Date:** _____

5. Consent Form:

AUTHORIZATION FOR RELEASE OR EXCHANGE OF INFORMATION

This form when completed and signed by you, authorizes _____ to release protected health information from you/your child's clinical record to the person that you designate. It may also allow information of a clinical, medical or educational nature to be exchanged between the two parties if so indicated below.

I authorize Newtown Recovery and Resiliency Team to release and exchange information regarding _____ DOB: _____ to the following party. This information should only be released to or obtained from:

_____

I am requesting NRRT to release this information for the following reasons:

_____

Care Coordination: _____

This authorization shall remain in effect until _____

Revoked: _____

You have the right to revoke this authorization, in writing, at any time by sending notification to the office.

I understand that information used or disclosed pursuant to the authorization may be subject to re-disclosure by the recipient of the information and no longer protected by the HIPAA privacy rule.

_____   _____

Signature of client or parent if a minor   *Date*

These documents and personal intake interviews were critical to our success because they blended the best practices of social work with standard medical and nursing assessments. There are many examples of psychosocial assessments that can be adapted as a care coordinator screening tool. It is important to decide what information will most inform your clinical decisions and your reports about recovery projections and forecasts. Our assessment screen allowed us not only to match clients with providers, but to track progress and provide a comprehensive follow-through program so that we could determine the effectiveness of treatment options.

IN SUMMARY

When caring for individuals who are experiencing distress on a profound level, you want to match your process for responding with an equally profound intensive service. We looked at taking a form of case management and ramping it up. We called this care coordination. We provided assessment and resources for care with a high level of accessibility, nurturing, clinical expertise, and follow through. This model eliminated the possibility of people falling through the cracks.

We believe we had a high level of success matching individuals to the right treatments and health care needs, while minimizing risk and increasing the probability that recovery would lead to ultimate resiliency. Creating this model involved thoughtful attention to every aspect of the work, including hiring the right coordinators, providing training and education, choosing assessment tools, and setting up a trauma-informed workspace.

CHAPTER FIVE

THE POLITICS
OF RECOVERY

The emotional nature of devastation impassions politics and breeds divides. While at first the shared experience of the tragedy brings a sense of unity, it also spotlights opposing perspectives. These differences often lead to a culture of choosing sides or conflicting agendas. This chapter contains examples of challenges I faced as I forged our recovery efforts. While these examples are negative in nature, my intent in sharing them is simply to show that this work is not without its pitfalls. There will likely be moments when you question your approach and feel as though your work would be better served with clearer systems in place, or if everyone could check their emotions at the door. That is not likely to happen. But if you start with an awareness of the challenges, they are that much easier to navigate when they surface.

The ideal situation occurs when community leaders turn a tragedy into an anchoring event to bring people together. Yet even with the best of intentions, the dynamics of a trauma may result in fracturing within the community. In my experience, leaders either promote or inhibit healing with their messages.

When I began working in Newtown, there were many issues that evoked strong feelings and divides among different factions of the community. Both formal and informal discussions were held about whether boundaries should be set regarding advocacy for national causes such as gun control, or for local concerns like school safety. Views differed about the inclusion of victims' names and faces in news reports; some feared that they would be used to market a cause. Besides these national issues, there were also opinions about the management of recovery efforts by local municipalities and organizations. For example, Newtown officials debated concepts for a victims' memorial, what to do with the perpetrator's home, how best to utilize private donations, and how federal aid should be disbursed to impacted communities. Opinions on how much the community had progressed in its healing and resiliency were especially contentious. Status reports from experts brought in to help with recovery often met resistance. Residents had begun to express their mental health needs more clearly, alerting us to a laundry list of gaps in services and deep-seated frustrations. I assumed political leaders would welcome this information and work to address these issues by closing the gaps. Instead, they often preferred to minimize the demand for treatment and programming, as if they didn't want the public to know the healing was ongoing. At these times, it felt like the people who should have been supporting me were adding new challenges.

Often, the opinions and decisions from the town government differed from the viewpoints of individuals seeking support. This occasionally led to a public perception that there was inadequate support for recovery efforts. Had less energy been spent creating the facade that everyone was taken care of and doing well, my work discussing needs and developing effective responses would have been much easier. It seemed like I constantly had to convince town leaders that it was okay to say trauma-related issues would take many years to address.

Having these differences remain unresolved may contribute to fracturing, and without a doubt the dynamic interferes with your agenda. You may deliver a message you believe to be positive, but find out that some interpreted your intent differently. There will likely be instances when you have to accept that your day will end with a few new bruises.

These experiences remind you not to leave town leaders out of the recovery programming. Imagine holding a high-level position in a community. Your job is busy and your responsibilities include a broad range of tasks. A massive tragedy hits the community, requiring both immediate and long-term responses. It was a tragedy that no one could have prepared for. There is no protocol. There are no assigned personnel to address needs. No budget. The problems are vast. Residents feel broken, and the whole world is watching.

Leaders are rarely educated in trauma treatment, the trauma trajectory, or community recovery. In fact, it's safe to assume that town leaders are experiencing some level of trauma themselves. Often enough, leaders in the community feel an obligation to present a picture of wholeness and control, even if that is not the case. There might be a fear of appearing vulnerable when they believe their role is to hold the community together. Or there might be a compulsion to have all the answers even when they do not. Under close scrutiny from the media, they may feel responsible to get "back to normal" quickly. When I stepped into my role as the NRRT leader, I assumed the Newtown political leadership had a strong grasp of their constituents' needs and were moving recovery efforts forward. The intent was always there, and they were doing their best, but they were learning as they went.

As a clinician I understand that those in prominent positions, such as an elected official or department head, will experience some level of vicarious trauma, which can result in exhaustion and burnout. When they are unable to alleviate others' pain or immediately fix concerns, their behavior may be interpreted as lacking in compassion and empathy, making them appear "checked out" or overwhelmed. For those grieving the loss of a child or family member, emotions run high, and leaders often bear the brunt of these emotions. I heard from residents and employees who felt their leaders were not present at the level they had expected. A perceived unwillingness to embrace their needs was mentioned. Some groups talked about a breakdown in communication and a lack of daily presence. Some said, "We brought these concerns forward but were told to focus on the positives and that there are plenty of resources—even though those resources have not been effective."

CREATING EFFECTIVE OVERSIGHT

I also experienced difficulty with my volunteer board of directors. The board was in place before I was hired. It included eight individuals who were looked at as leaders in Newtown and represented several facets of the community, including clergy, business owners, first selectman (equivalent to a city councilman), the school superintendent, an administrator from the local hospital, and a local foundation head, among others. Most of the members wore several hats, sat on other boards, and held prominent roles in the community. For instance, the chairman of the board was also the town's political leader, the first selectwoman. The hospital professional was also on the distribution committee for the Newtown Community Foundation.

As appreciative as I was for some semblance of guidance, I believe this board struggled to define itself as either an advisory board or an oversight board. In my experience an advisory board is meant to provide direction and support for an organization's programming and decisions as they relate to the community recovery work. It champions the team's effort. The members should promote and participate in events and bring suggestions and feedback to the table. In contrast, an oversight board is meant to assess and evaluate the outcomes of the recovery work; it provides both fiscal auditing and management accountability.

When there is uncertainty about the fundamental role of the board (and subsequently, one's relationship to it), that dynamic can be less than effective, and frustrating to deal with. When I delivered an update or monthly report to my board, there was confusion as to whether the concerns they raised were driven by other positions they held, or community recovery. Often, I wasn't sure if we were meeting for the board to gather information and interject with concerns drawn from their other roles, or to champion our team's efforts. This resulted in many long meetings and lengthy discussions about individual facets of the reports, but not much guidance or assistance.

Worse, because the chairwoman was the town's political leader, it was hard for other board members to break rank with her. Even when I thought I had made headway toward a strong connection with some board members, if my updates conflicted with the opinion of the chairwoman, I would not receive open support from anyone. While I seemed to have the full trust of this board, throughout my tenure I came to understand that there was not always true transparency if my agenda conflicted with the chairwoman's. As a result, I adopted a strategy by which I treated the board as an oversight organization rather than an advisory group. I reported on the team's activities and upcoming goals. I provided data reports and case examples. I included successes and challenges. I asked for what I needed in terms of support, but did not count on the board as a driving force to promote our work or success.

I share this experience because being prepared to encounter similar challenges can serve as a form of self-awareness (do not take it personally). If you create the right processes, procedures, and administrative structures before a disaster happens, then these concepts can be carefully thought out and evaluated before being put in place.

Having a governing board for mental health efforts may not always be appropriate. However, if that is the structure you are working under, the board should have a clearly identified role. In my experience, the most effective board of directors attends your events and sees themselves as the steward of your team's recovery work. This type of board should include individuals who do not necessarily have a seat on other boards that serve in response to the tragedy. Political leaders should be invited to meetings, but should not sit as the chair.

RELUCTANCE WITHIN THE TOWN SYSTEM

You may experience your own conflicts with those at the top, like I did. While this was the exception, when the conflict did occur I had to make decisions about the importance of pushing forward despite the conflict, believing that the outcomes would far outweigh the challenges. When I presented a comprehensive offsite program to address the expressed needs of Sandy Hook teachers and forge a path for continued recovery, I met pushback from town leadership. They offered a thousand reasons why it wouldn't be successful, ranging from a lack of funds for class coverage while the teachers attended the event, to limited transportation. These challenges could have been easily resolved, yet met complete negativity. When I met with another town department head to discuss top-down policies to foster recovery and develop a more effective communications approach with its rank-and-file staff, I was told, "It won't matter. The culture won't change." I engaged for many hours with an esteemed recovery organization to help service an impacted group that had said it wouldn't trust anyone else, but leadership scuttled the proposal before it was even submitted.

Why say "no thanks" to an offer to participate in trainings crafted to meet gaps the town was unable to fill? Why block efforts to bring in new voices that would help the recovery process? What you may find while doing this work is that the emotional exhaustion and pain make it difficult for some to accept help, let alone engage in recovery.

Some of the necessary work was to resolve long-standing interdepartmental tensions and repair mistakes that occurred early on in the management of the tragedy. Some of these problems had resulted in healing professionals, town employees, and organizations stepping away from the recovery effort prematurely due to disagreements on needs, service provisions, and/or control over the clinical delivery. Some providers felt that their services were compromised due to conflicting agendas with the town government. This included clinicians who felt that their expertise was overridden or unvalued. While I could not turn back time to fix what was already done, I had to overcome the barriers and resistance that resulted from the mistakes. Within the town government, communication between municipal departments was breaking down before the tragedy. Afterward, these cracks became gaping holes. There may have been some awareness of the issues beforehand, yet new interdepartmental conflicts also appeared in the face of the tragedy. Some of the issues were acknowledged, and we were considered a welcome aid in resolving them. Others were not, and we met resistance in our attempts to address those.

As a recovery leader you will have to decide which issues you are willing to engage with in spite of the resistance. I continued to offer my insights and share the feedback I received from residents at strategic meetings with other departments or organizations. The point was to bring awareness to the challenges others faced. I hoped to create momentum to discuss these challenges and work towards addressing them. But I see now that although I approached our work with a can-do attitude, many of the individuals I engaged with were already traumatized and exhausted.

I was not the first to offer assistance and find that progress was slow. For every well-intentioned effort, there were some who benefited and others who were not ready to change. They wished and hoped we could just return to the days before the shooting and resume business as usual.

Approach your leaders with sensitivity to their culture and the nuances of their roles. A police chief must return to everyday policing and manage his department without appearing vulnerable. A school principal must resume a culture in which educating students is a priority that cannot be compromised. The governing leaders must keep the town running. A member of the clergy must lead their congregation with faith and hope. And most importantly, as well as most challenging, as a mental health expert you must do your best to create relationships that let them know it's okay to be vulnerable or express weariness. Communicate that you are there to help and will assist in easing that burden.

BEWARE THE SUVS

To complicate matters, Newtown was immediately inundated by volunteers and spontaneous uninvited visitors (SUVs) with no one to manage them. Before we arrived on the scene, hundreds of these well-meaning people had come into the Sandy Hook/Newtown community thinking they could help.

Some SUVs provided services that made themselves feel better but did not help the community because the services did not match its needs or use best practice models. Some promised an outcome they could not deliver, for example claiming they would remain in Newtown for ongoing support when in fact they had a limited timeframe in the community. Sometimes it was the level of support that they did not have the capacity to sustain. Worse, some approached this tragedy as an opportunity to increase their exposure or seek other personal gains. In the most extreme cases, SUVs believed they could provide a service and receive reimbursement without following the protocols set by the town.

Without a manager to vet and coordinate the SUVs, harm may occur and distrust can grow. It's unsurprising that this scenario can cause a breakdown in communication between the community leaders, residents, and recovery professionals. Consequently, leaders may become skeptical of outsiders. An uneasiness and lack of cooperation can develop between even the most well-intentioned professionals and the community.

To minimize or reverse community distrust, your town will need to put systems in place to vet future volunteer organizations and treatment professionals. There should be a designated individual or team that creates a protocol system that includes evaluating professional credentials and the value and quality of services offered. In Newtown, our team assumed this responsibility. We met with many providers, asked them questions about their practices and credentials, and noted client reviews of their experiences. But because we came onto the scene a year and a half after the tragedy, there was a lot of catch-up work. This can be avoided if a system is in place.

WORKING WITHIN A FRACTURED COMMUNITY

I have illustrated some ways in which fracturing occurs and the impact it has on recovery work. With an awareness of this phenomenon you can begin to bridge divides and work with leaders and their agendas to determine how to meet the community's needs.

I finished my work in Newtown feeling like I could have achieved three times as much if I had not encountered resistance at seemingly every turn. While it would have been easy to be negative about this, I eventually realized that meeting resistance is a part of the work. It results naturally from the pain and should be seen as a part of the healing process.

When encountering resistance, ask yourself why it might be occurring. Evaluating the rationale behind an underlying resistance may help you work toward a more cooperative culture. Perhaps you can be the voice that reframes the situation and offers resolution or options that satisfy both sides. Or you may be the leader who educates others on why a divide has occurred and opens discussion on how to bridge differences without furthering frustration and pain.

Next, address the leadership's own issues surrounding trauma and complicated grief. Include town leaders in as many aspects of recovery work as is appropriate. Hold special programming sessions for them. Ask for their presence at your events or in promoting your events. Sometimes this requires you have to check their schedules to accommodate them or create a scenario in which it is difficult for them not to attend. While it is hard to assess the benefit of increased awareness of trauma and grief impacts among town leaders, I frequently heard our first selectman make statements to the public and media that indicated an increased level of understanding.

Also be aware of how you present yourself and your particular role. Communicate awareness that their job is challenging and different from yours. Build trust by always being the ultimate professional, a person who does not perpetuate or engage in fracturing. Do not continue to put energy into meetings or agendas that are counterproductive.

IN SUMMARY

It is understandable that town leaders might go to great lengths to avoid feeling uncomfortable in the aftermath of a tragedy. They desperately want their community to be whole again, and feel tasked with the daunting job of leading their constituency through an unspeakable situation. Every day presents new challenges. It must be particularly difficult for leaders to find themselves in a situation that they cannot make better. The result is a desire to portray an unrealistic picture of the impact in an attempt to make everyone feel more comfortable. However, we learned that resiliency truly occurs when you are able to walk through the uncomfortable situations and get to the other side. Embracing this concept is hard work.

CHAPTER SIX

FOLLOWING
THE MONEY

Recovery and resiliency work is always expensive. Addressing future needs for enhanced security, recovery preparedness, and capacity building to cover the changed landscape after a tragedy is more often than not beyond what any town or community can plan for. Luckily, there are many ways to access money. In fact, one of the unexpected consequences of disaster is the influx of money into a town. Having systems in place to deal with its proper distribution can eliminate stress and added complications.

Conversations surrounding money can be challenging and awkward, even frustrating at times. However, they are important to embrace as a part of the process. Even if your training and expertise are in providing clinical support, you cannot divorce yourself from the business side of the work. So it is best to prepare to navigate the money trail.

We were fortunate to receive significant financial donations in the wake of the Newtown shooting because the heartbreaking tragedy was widely covered. In total, more than $12 million was raised. It is impossible to determine how much money will be enough—recovery is expensive and having financial resources readily available can eliminate tremendous burdens and treatment barriers. However, donation money comes with its own set of challenges.

People all around the world generously sent in money, which was collected by the local United Way chapter. A support fund was then created and held at the Newtown Savings Bank. The original fund was established for undesignated financial donations, money that could be used as needed for individual and community recovery purposes. Later, the town also received a supplemental grant from the Department of Justice for treatment and health reimbursements.

Within two months of the school shooting, a second organization was formed: the Newtown/Sandy Hook Community Foundation (NSHCF). This was a separate entity from the town government—an independent nonprofit mandated to create a reserve of funds that could support operations and activities that addressed short- and long-term needs of individuals and the community arising from the tragic event. The funds were raised locally and included the United Way donations, which would now be controlled with community input. Again, it is impossible to put a dollar value on what might be needed until the scope and impact of the tragedy is assessed. There may be ongoing fundraising needs for years to come. However, it is important to manage the money with professionalism and transparency.

The foundation was led by an executive director, a board of directors, and a distribution committee that made disbursement recommendations to the board. The NSHCF had a variety of community members on its board and distribution committee, including those who were most impacted. These members represented a balance of individuals qualified to review requests and evaluate needs—a parent who lost his child, the head of psychiatry at a local hospital, an accountant, a professional counselor, a clergy member, and others.

It takes a tremendous amount of work, thoughtfulness, and collaboration to manage funds with professionalism, ethics, integrity, and transparency. By the time the NRRT was formed, the management of much of the money coming into Newtown for health and wellness recovery efforts, as well as the money flowing out, was managed by the NSHCF. This arrangement proved extremely valuable, efficient, and ethical in its activities and responsibilities. It removed the challenges of fund distribution from the town government and created a sense of fairness and efficacy in the process. All requests for funds received thoughtful consideration.

One goal for the NSHCF was to ensure that funds would be in place for the long-term health and wellness and mental health needs of those most impacted. Each community will have to define what "long-term" means as befits its funds and needs. For Newtown, one marker of success was if funds could be available to support the youngest children who were at the Sandy Hook School that day through their high school graduations. This would be approximately fourteen years. The NSHCF created guidelines for determining which populations could receive funding and developed standards for treatment modalities and reimbursement amounts in order to have the money last as long as possible.

While NSHCF focused on health and wellness requests, other groups were able to assist with basic needs, such as outstanding bills to run a household or pay for a school trip. Several grassroots foundations, including nonprofit and religious organizations, also launched. Their fundraising efforts yielded money that also went toward recovery work. For instance, The Sandy Hook Promise and Walnut Hill Church were two organizations that readily made funds available to families impacted by the tragedy who were unable to pay for mental health services or basic needs to keep their family afloat. Other organizations, like the local Lion's Club and Sandy Hook Memorial Foundation, turned monies that they raised over to the NSHCF for distribution. The organizations all had parameters and stipulated what they believed to be appropriate requests based on donor intent.

FINANCIAL BEST PRACTICES

It's important for communities to have a designated place where the money will sit and a managing body to set the criteria for how it's going to be spent. This requires addressing the following questions. The answers will differ for every community and should be communicated with clarity and transparency to the public.

- Will the money be invested? If so, how?
- Who will receive funds?
- How long does the money need to last? What percentage of funds should be preserved for future needs?
- What percentage of funds should go to individual recovery needs?
- What percentage of funds should be allocated for training programs, recovery programs, or community programs?

- What are the criteria for eligibility?
- What are acceptable requests?
- What are acceptable reimbursement rates?
- What is the protocol or mechanism for requests?
- What is the protocol or mechanism for approval?
- What are the guidelines for provider requests and submissions?
- Who will make these decisions?
- Who will evaluate and develop this protocol?
- Who will determine if there is an exception to the rules or an appeal process?
- How will reimbursements be disbursed?
- How will reimbursements be recorded?

THE NRRT ROLE IN ALLOCATING FINANCIAL RESOURCES

Shortly after accepting my position, I learned that the Connecticut State Office of Victim Services (OVS), which was in charge of evaluating and assessing requests for financial assistance, would turn this role over to my team. OVS is a Department of Justice office that supports families with the emotional and financial impacts of crimes in all US states and territories. A school shooting meets this criterion. The state OVS office had already begun to manage donations and allocate money to the NSHCF, which then transferred evaluation duties to the NRRT. Distributions to eligible victim families were made early on. The remainder was earmarked for short- and long-term community recovery needs.

We were asked to assume the role of assessing and making decisions for individual requests—in essence to be gatekeepers to recovery resources. This meant that while we were not technically allocating funds, we facilitated and processed those requests for the town. The requests that came in were widespread, yet most were mental health related. Others were due to financial hardship—an individual losing his job or having a diminished capacity to work because of an emotional injury related to the tragedy.

A major part of the work was deciding who met the criteria established by the NSHCF Foundation, OVS, or other organizations that raised money for financial reimbursement. In fact, acting as a liaison between the money and those individual community members requesting financial assistance became one of our team's primary roles. It involved determining whether their challenges or treatment needs were due to the tragedy. The team would then determine where to access the funds, and ensure that all prerequisites (Had it been submitted to their insurance first? Is the provider able to bill insurance? Is the request capped at a certain amount? Does the request fall under our accepted list of treatment or wellness options?) were met. A request for a gym membership might go to the Newtown-Sandy Hook School Foundation because it would fall under their mission to promote health and wellness. A request for money to pay a utility bill or make outstanding mortgage payments would be sent to a local church or the Sandy Hook Promise Foundation. An individual request for a specialized program or service that did not fall under the stated criteria might fit into a category supported by OVS. The State Office of Victim Services maintained trusts that were exclusively available to victims' loved ones and witness children's families.

The project manager and I quickly realized we would need a tracking system to monitor where the money was being spent and to evaluate requests, trends, and needs for insight into what funds might be needed in the future. The Department of Justice did not indicate a need for any such system in the grant guidelines, but I realized that ideas and reporting needs would become apparent as we became entrenched in the work. We needed a system to collect demographics, clinical data, and reimbursement information—a hybrid between accounting software and an outcome database. The data system we wanted would collect request and allocation data, process information from insurance companies or third party distributors, and create anonymous reports for our board and stakeholders who tracked the use of funds.

Because my team was the first of its kind, we had to create our system from scratch. We could not initially find a database that matched our needs and budget, so we worked with a software company to create one. We then exported the data on funds previously distributed by OVS over to the new system.

The NRRT project manager took charge of this data system. The care coordinators assumed the role of assessing requests and fed the data to the project manager. She in turn uploaded the information, tracked third-party reimbursement offsets, and created a report twice monthly that was sent to the NSHCF for checks to be cut. In our small community, distributions averaged $50,000 a month.

The process began each time an individual came to us for assistance. They would meet with a care coordinator to request treatment resources, and the care coordinator would assess them using a modified psychosocial assessment. During this phase, the care coordinator would ask questions that helped determine if the need was directly related to the tragedy. Because the policy was that all requests for clinical treatment had to be submitted to a third-party insurance provider first, care coordinators educated the individual on this process and sometimes called their insurance company to determine benefits.

Behind the scenes, every service provider who received reimbursement funds was also registered in the database. The care coordinator worked closely with the project manager to secure these registrations. Part of the process for service providers included vetting. Were they delivering a service that was clinically recognized? Was their fee within the customary fee structure that the foundation accepted? Were they appropriately licensed and/or certified?

Before a reimbursement was authorized and distributed by the NSHCF, the individual or provider had to produce an explanation of benefits form that showed the service had been denied by an insurance company. But because many clinical providers in Newtown did not participate with third-party payers, this piece of documentation was not always necessary.

My team followed the requests and funds for each individual. If an explanation of benefits form was absent, my project manager followed up to secure it. She kept a paper file of these documents and only entered the appropriate information into the database. When there was a question as to whether a request met the established criteria, or if an exception might be made, we submitted a rationale to the foundation, and their distribution committee made the final decision.

This system was extremely efficient. In almost all instances, when a request was made and an invoice submitted, the reimbursement check was processed within two weeks. This is extremely important when you realize that the individual asking for help is likely struggling with bills and the cumbersome process of working with an insurance company. He may not have the capacity or energy to navigate these systems on his own. And this factor alone can be a deterrent to getting help. Treatment providers may be reluctant to provide service if they do not know if and when a reimbursement will arrive. The fact that there was an efficient local system in place, with caring professionals bearing the burden of ensuring that treatment bills were paid, was of tremendous relief to many.

There were other benefits to our system as well. If a provider's fees were out of line with what was deemed customary, we advocated that the provider accept the lower reimbursement rate. If the provider had difficulty submitting paperwork, we assisted them. At times individuals would walk into our center with an armful of invoices and insurance letters, asking our team to help organize and make sense of the mess, which we did.

We gathered vital information on where money was going and provided input on how to adjust the criteria so existing funds were sustained for future needs. At times, this meant delivering the difficult message that a request didn't meet the NSHCF criteria. For instance, the care coordinator may have determined that a request in fact pertained to a preexisting condition unrelated to the tragedy. Or an individual might request an alternative treatment or strategy that was not approved by the NSHCF.

Lastly, if necessary, we arranged for funds from our other sources. In these instances, we also had to provide the information showing that the request held up to donor intent and that only those individuals who qualified received what was allotted. Our care coordinators could make phone calls and submit requests to entities such as churches or local organizations that had pledged to help.

The following form was used in the NRRT office to track financial issues per client:

STATUS

Pending _____   Paid _____   Approved _____

Chk # _____   Submitted _____   Date Pd _____

REQUEST FOR ASSISTANCE
Collaborative Recovery Fund Assessment Form

Received Date: _____   Family ID: _____

Have you applied to this program previously?   ❑ Yes ❑ No ❑ Unknown

If yes, have you received assistance from the fund? ❑ Yes ❑ No ❑ Pending

═══════════════ **Applicant Information:** ═══════════════

_____

First Name   *MI*   *Last Name*

═══════════════ **Assistance Applying For:** ═══════════════

Please be aware that all payment(s) will be made directly to provider(s), except for prescription reimbursement, which will be provided directly to the applicant in the form of a check. For auditing purposes, the Fund requires at least $20.00 worth of prescription expenses before considering reimbursement.

❑ **Mental Health** *traditional mental health out-of-pocket costs not covered by other financial resources. Must provide copy(ies) of receipts showing payment or an itemized bill.*

Dates of Service: _____

Provider: _____

REQUEST FOR ASSISTANCE
Collaborative Recovery Fund Assessment Form (cont)

❑ **Prescription(s)**   *must provide the original pharmacy printout*

Dates of Service: _____

Name of Pharmacy: _____

Provider: _____

❑ **Health & Wellness**   *must-traditional therapeutic interventions deemed an important extension of treatment. Must provide copy(ies) of medical note of receipts showing payment or an itemized bill.*

Dates of Service: _____

Provider: _____

❑ Acupuncture/Chiropractic Care   ❑ Equine-Assisted Therapy (EAT)

❑ Social/Emotional support & enrichment activities for children

❑ Physical health & fitness activities   ❑ Massage

❑ Emotional Freedom Techniques (EFT)/Tapping

❑ Other Alternative:_____

❑ **Other**   *must provide copy(ies) of receipts showing payment or an itemized bill*

Dates of Service: _____

Provider: _____

_____   _____
Authorization Signature   *Date Signed*

The Emotional Challenges of Accessing Resources

Money can cause further fracturing within an emotionally impacted community. There will be expressions of gratitude for financial assistance, yet also complaints of unfairness, frustration, and hurt when a request cannot be honored. We would hear: "But my neighbor got approval for a summer camp. The request I'm making is just as therapeutic." "Why do so many people get financial assistance who were not directly impacted? Shouldn't the funds exclusively go to those who were directly impacted, like my family?" "Why should I have to submit this to my insurance company first? Haven't I been through enough?" And: "I heard you have millions of dollars available. Why can't you approve this request?"

This is why having strong criteria set by a collaboration of individuals is important. You cannot avoid setting limits, and there will always be some who disagree with your decisions. You do not want money issues to slow down the healing process, though. This is why our team provided assistance to find alternative resources for treatment or funding when necessary.

FUNDING COMMUNITY MENTAL HEALTH PROGRAMS

I have highlighted our formula of assisting with individual fund requests. But this was just a portion of financial need. Recovery efforts should occur on both the micro- and macro-levels. A comprehensive recovery effort includes community programs, trainings, and workshops. On the micro-level, we assisted and evaluated individual and family needs. On the macro-level, we evaluated the demand for programming that would address the unique needs of specialized groups like first responders, teachers, or clinicians. Following evaluation, it was our job to create or secure resources and coordinate or sponsor targeted programs, all of which required significant funding.

The recovery leader is required to find funds, raise funds, and negotiate for financial needs. Our DOJ Consequence Management Grant did not include discretionary funds for programming and recovery work; it covered salaries and expenses for our job duties. That meant that whenever I decided to provide a specific program or service, such as hiring an outside presenter to address the entire community, I had to determine how to pay for it.

The NSHCF reserved a portion of its managed funds for community programming and set up a process by which individuals and organizations could write a simple grant to request financial assistance. I also sought funds from the parent-teacher association, a local police union, and two nonprofit organizations, the Sandy Hook Promise and the Parent Connection. I presented needs to a large church that had raised money to help and donated generously when appropriate. I collaborated with community leaders to find angel donors who had stepped forward to provide financial support for community efforts. I negotiated with presenters, local venues, and more. I also collaborated with other organizations that had budgets to support a program.

When we presented an idea for a program, there were often financial concerns for the group we targeted. For example, when I wanted to run a program for first responders, we realized they would only attend if we paid their overtime. Was there money in the education budget for substitute teachers if we invited school personnel to participate in an offsite program during a school day?

As a recovery professional you quickly learn that resources are always limited and will likely not cover all the community's recovery needs. Becoming adept at identifying and tapping resources beyond what the town can provide relieves some of the pressure that your leaders experience.

Knowing where to ask for funds, and getting a firm financial commitment to support programming, is extremely important when reporting on activities and goals. Otherwise, even the most thoughtful programs may be pipedreams. You also risk creating more anxiety for town leaders if they sense they have to raise money to support your programs on their own.

Being able to present a program plan with funding intact will foster goodwill. If you are constantly asking your leaders for money, they will become wary of you. I quickly realized that whatever program I wanted to develop, I needed to find independent funding for. When I presented the plan in the whole package, I had a greater chance of buy-in from town leaders.

For instance, we created a daylong retreat for the Sandy Hook Elementary School staff that included their spouses and significant others. The program was a series of experiential mini-workshops on trauma reaction and wellness strategies. The day included clinical group offerings for family members to discuss their roles and needs, and it culminated in a meal for everyone to celebrate the value of individual and collective support. This was meant to jumpstart future programming. Our grant did not include money to cover a program like this, so I raised the funds through a request to the school PTA.

We created a yearlong recovery and support program for the town's first responders, which required over $400,000 in funding. Less than a third of that amount was allocated in the grant; the rest had to be raised privately. We also created smaller programs for clinicians, municipal staff, and the general public. Some of these efforts were financially supported by a grant from the NSHCF.

MANAGING NON-MONETARY DONATIONS

Newtown was also flooded with material items donated from all over the world—thousands of teddy bears, toys, blankets, artwork, art supplies, gift cards, and clothing. Well-meaning individuals, groups, religious organizations, and companies sent them. In reality some were value-added, but most were not. These items needed to be stored and distributed, and the quantity was obviously disproportionate to the number of individuals who might have benefited from them.

It's wonderful that people want to make a kind gesture of goodwill in response to a tragedy. But it's best to recognize that material goods need to be managed, and in our case this became a real issue. Most communities do not have an employee or two who can put aside other responsibilities to address this task. The local post office was inundated with extra work managing the flow of donations. The town had to rent a warehouse when existing storage places filled to capacity. And I clearly remember a local church rectory having donation boxes pile up in its hallways, which everyone had to navigate through.

A teddy bear or blanket didn't necessarily provide a sense of comfort, either. Supplying children with extra toys was not always the message the parents wanted to send to their children, and could come with its own set of questions and issues. While the artwork was heartfelt, there were only so many places to display the pieces, and eventually they become an unwanted reminder of the tragedy.

As you may expect, the monetary donations were the most valuable. There was a clear way to manage the money and appropriate it for healing and recovery purposes. This is not meant to place a negative veil over the offers and intentions of others, but rather to illustrate the needs of personnel to appropriately manage and prepare for these expected responses. Staying ahead of the expected influx of goods and services can eliminate a great deal of stress on an already stretched community.

IN SUMMARY

Knowing where funds are and how to navigate this landscape will be an integral part of the work. Understand that money is necessary to achieve certain outcomes but comes with its own set of responsibilities and stressors. Finally, tracking the expenditures and allocations, and forecasting future community needs, should be a priority. Clarity and transparency is necessary, along with thoughtfulness and professional scrutiny. It is extremely helpful to have a designated foundation or organization whose main function is to manage funds. Along with this, it is important to have independent committees that meet regularly to make individual decisions regarding the criteria for fund distribution.

PART II

Individualizing Recovery

CHAPTER SEVEN

THERAPIES AND PROGRAMMING THAT WORK

The goal in trauma treatment is not to erase the memory, but to integrate the experience in healthy, adaptive ways. The result can provide growth and positive change. This is resiliency: managing symptoms and gaining a sense of empowerment over the impact. Resiliency is the ability to live in the present without being incapacitated by memories of the traumatic event.

While the process is different for everyone, we know there are common feelings that follow a traumatic experience, which include helplessness, a loss of control or power, and a profound sense of isolation. This often translates into feeling unsafe in your own body, your own thoughts, and in relationships with others. Trauma can leave a person feeling like they are, or want to be, invisible. On the surface, isolating yourself may appear safer than exposing yourself to being vulnerable or feeling overwhelmed with emotion.

If not treated effectively, trauma changes from a defining moment in an individual's life to an adverse transformation of that person's identity. When this happens, it is characterized by negative maladaptive behaviors and fraught with emotional distress. This can translate into emotional, physical, and relational dysfunction. However, with appropriate treatment and support, an individual can view themselves as a trauma survivor with the ability to move forward and enjoy positive resiliency.

THE CRITICAL NATURE OF COMMUNITY

Trauma often impacts relationships with others, so it is important to build or rebuild personal and relational support systems. A connection to others is vital to the healing process. For many individuals who walked through our door, simply meeting with a care coordinator and establishing a trusting relationship with them was the first step in overcoming isolation. While it's true that no one can understand what it's like to walk in someone else's shoes, particularly after a devastating event, patiently building nurturing supports can happen. Yet it's important to meet someone where they are and work at their pace.

Before suggesting any therapies, our care coordinators would spend time building a relationship. They would do this in a number of ways:

- Take a walk to discuss the individual's needs outside the office.
- Meet with the affected person's family members.
- Attend a community event with the individual.

- Call ahead to a group or organization to pave the way for them to walk in with minimal anxiety.
- Explore their spiritual beliefs and opportunities to engage with those avenues.
- Meet with a teacher, school nurse, or social worker to build a strong support network.

Feeling nurtured and having a fundamental connection to others cannot be substituted in the healing process. Building or strengthening a personal support system is often the first step towards resiliency. Outside of therapy, care coordinators would encourage clients to engage more with their community in order to build resiliency. Their suggestions included:

- Participating in a social community event with a friend or family member.
- Reengaging with or joining a sports team.
- Partaking in an activity that was creative, rhythmic, or had a high degree of sensory input to help regulate the brain, such as running, art therapy, or music therapy.

A MULTI-LAYERED THERAPEUTIC APPROACH

Treating trauma does not come with a one-size-fits-all solution. Reaction to trauma is individualized, and the trajectory can be difficult to predict. Factors, including a person's age, past exposure to trauma, available social support, culture, present stressors and coping skills, individual and family psychiatric history, comorbid maladaptive behaviors such as addiction history, physical health, and general emotional functioning influence the trauma response, and subsequently the ability to heal and embrace a pathway to resiliency.

Because trauma leaves an imprint on the body, we found the most effective strategy was to help individuals address the body's connection to the mind. When a person's sense of safety has been threatened, the body holds on to the memory and resulting pain. Not only can the trauma thus remain trapped in the body, creating persistent changes that manifest as unhealthy reactions, the perceived threat of danger can be retriggered, and symptoms surface. For many, the physical and emotional results of a traumatic event often last well after the event ended, as the nervous system remains primed and ready for self-defense.

Trauma impacts our emotional status and physical responses, and we have yet to identify a form of treatment that is effective by itself. In Newtown, we found the best results in a layered treatment approach. This may include clinical treatments as well as health and wellness practices. The reason is that many trauma survivors experience a change in their nervous system that disrupts the ability to feel grounded, which needs to be addressed *before* engaging in treatments that focus on processing the trauma. The practice of grounding should take place throughout the treatment process, and may be necessary throughout the individual's life span.

Treatments and lifestyle changes were prescribed simultaneously. Yoga classes and a gym membership were used to help regulate the nervous system, and somatic experiencing or cognitive behavioral therapy were integrated into work on processing the traumatic experience. When someone presented in a state of hyper-arousal, we focused on stabilization activities while making sure they had adequate supports and a safety plan during the process.

Many individuals would show up to our office in a state of acute distress, having not yet learned how to regulate or soothe these emotions. For some, just trying to verbalize emotions felt overwhelming. In these situations, our trauma specialist might begin the stabilization process by engaging the individual in a simple tapping exercise or mindful meditation. Some individuals sought assistance after completing one kind of behavioral therapeutic treatment because they were still symptomatic. We would determine what other treatments could be added or layered in to help relieve those symptoms and successfully move them through the healing process.

Many people were confused about treatment options, but didn't feel empowered to ask for help with understanding why a strategy or modality they had engaged in hadn't seemed to work. We decided to put together a guide and co-sponsor a community-wide event that showcased therapeutic practices. We printed this reference guide in booklet form with a glossy cover that everyone could take home. Then we invited practitioners to set up tables with information to answer questions and educate the public about what they did. There was a panel discussion highlighting a few practitioners and treatments. We had a morning and afternoon session to meet all scheduling needs. There was tremendous feedback; we heard people positively reference the event for a long time afterward.

Many new treatments and strategies have come to light since the Sandy Hook School shooting. Some of these include Peter Levine's Somatic Experiencing, Bessel van der Kolk's work with traumatic stress, Eric Gentry's *Forward-Facing Trauma Therapy*, Stephen Porges' Polyvagal

Theory, and Pat Ogden's *Trauma and the Body*. Your treatment guide will likely vary depending on the community setting, the nature of the tragedy, access to resources, and new best practice modalities.

THERAPIES OFFERED

Merriam-Webster defines *therapy* as "the treatment of physical or mental illnesses," yet that definition is in need of updating, since science has demonstrated that mental illnesses should not be seen as separate from the body. Currently, many highly researched mental health treatments target areas of the brain anatomy in which trauma and other issues are stored.

We often think of therapy as merely talking to a professional. While this traditional mode continues to be beneficial, different types of therapy and therapeutic treatments have recently emerged. What follows is a brief synopsis of current mental/brain health therapies that have shown therapeutic benefits in addressing trauma. A number of the treatments overlap in certain ways. It may take sampling more than one to find the best option.

Of course, finding the right treatment, and more importantly the right practitioner, is an individualized process. The right therapy or therapist for one person is not always the best fit for another. While each therapy listed has merits, none will be its most effective without, first and foremost, a positive connection between client and clinician. Technique has value, but the person applying the technique is even more valuable.

Lastly, because the Newtown incident directly impacted both children and adults, we had to find therapeutic options for both. Some children may respond best to an expressive therapy, like art, music, or play therapy, because they lack the language capacity to express their needs in talk therapy. Some may benefit from animal-assisted therapy if trust in relationships has eroded; an animal creates a non-threatening way to work on relational needs. We found that following a traumatizing event, engaging someone in creating a cohesive narrative is not always possible. In the early stages of reactivity, children and adults are not likely to have the capacity to retrieve information about the event that is therapeutically beneficial. The autonomic nervous system may not have reset, so creative and expressive therapies can be the right match at this stage.

Acupuncture

Acupuncture is an ancient practice rooted in traditional Chinese medicine, which takes a different view of healing. It focuses on energy flow and the existence of energetic pathways, called meridians, which correlate to health and well-being. When energy is blocked or stagnant, physical and emotional illness can occur. Acupuncturists stimulate certain points on the body, most often with a needle penetrating the skin, to alleviate pain or help treat various health conditions. In some states, a license is required in order to practice acupuncture.

An acupuncturist will access points on the body that may be blocked or not flowing correctly. Each of the points relates to certain health problems or body functions. Landmarks on the body are then located—using certain muscles or bones—to find the points in which to place the needles. After locating the points, needles are quickly tapped into the skin. Some may be placed deeper than others, depending on what the provider believes is needed to restore the flow of energy.

Scientific studies have shown acupuncture to be an effective treatment for PTSD and trauma-related illnesses. It can be powerful to reduce stress, pain, and even depression, and can create an emotional release when an individual is flooded with stress hormones. It can be in used in conjunction with more traditional methods, such as cognitive behavioral therapy (CBT). Generally, acupuncture serves to bring the body back in balance.

Aromatherapy

Aromatherapy uses plant materials and aromatic plant oils, including essential oils, and other aromatic compounds for the purpose of enhancing one's mood as well as cognitive, psychological, or physical well-being.

It is believed that the inhaled aroma from these essential oils stimulates brain function. They are inhaled either through diffusers or from individual bottles. Essential oils may also be absorbed through the skin or taken internally, as long as the bottle indicates that the oil is safe for ingestion.

Aromatherapy is used for a variety of applications, including pain relief, mood enhancement, stress relief, and increased cognitive function. Stress responses can activate an individual's hypothalamus gland, pituitary gland, and limbic system. When certain natural plant derivatives are absorbed through the nose and skin, they interact with these systems and can have a direct calming and regulating effect. When used in conjunction with other mindful therapies it often promotes the body's ability to respond to these activities with a greater intensity.

Art Therapy

Art therapy uses a person's creativity to help develop their physical and emotional health. It combines traditional techniques found in psychotherapy with the creativity of producing visual art. Trauma-informed art therapy takes into consideration how the mind and body respond to traumatic events, recognizing that symptoms are coping strategies rather than pathology. It has been determined that self-expression can frequently awaken innate problem-solving capacities.

Art therapists are trained professionals who have a master's degree in art therapy. Artistic theories combined with clinical techniques are used to enhance the healing effect the creative process has on the client. The therapist is aware of the body's reactions to stressful events and/or memories and can thus incorporate sensory-based artistic activities.

People of all ages can benefit from trauma-informed art therapy, particularly those experiencing such issues as anxiety, depression, addiction, and trauma. This therapy approach is helpful for those who prefer focusing on another task while discussing complex issues verbally. Using art to express emotion accesses both visually-stored memory and body memory. Not only does it enable people to create images, but the use of art materials such as clay and paint can reconnect them to physical sensation. Making art with a professional art therapist can break the barriers of traditional language and create a process to express and reflect when experiencing life challenges such as illness or trauma. Art therapy can be a conduit to increased self-awareness, build coping skills, and reduce stress related to a traumatic experience, particularly when an individual's cognitive abilities are compromised.

Brainspotting

Brainspotting is designed to help access, process, and overcome trauma, negative emotions, and pain, including psychologically-induced pain. Evidence demonstrates that trauma is stored in the brain, thereby altering the way in which the brain works by interfering with emotion, memory, and physical health. By working on the limbic system, brainspottiing attempts to access both the physical and emotional aspects of negative emotions.

Brainspotting allows therapists to access emotions on a deeper level and to target the physical effects of trauma. A "brainspot" is an eye position that tends to activate a traumatic memory or painful emotion. The motto of brainspotting is: "where you look affects how you will feel." For many, looking left or right or up and down will trigger activation points. During a session, a therapist will help the client position their eyes in a way that enables them to target the source of the negative emotions.

Brainspotting has been used with promising results in trauma therapy and the treatment of PTSD. It can help people recovering from injuries and health problems, as well as issues such as motivation and attention. And since many everyday psychological issues, like anger and difficulty concentrating, can be caused by trauma, brainspotting may be effective when those concerns are trauma related. It can also be an effective treatment for those who are reluctant to seek traditional therapy, as the focus is on the brain rather than the person's feelings.

Cognitive Behavioral Therapy (CBT)

Cognitive behavioral therapy stems from the belief that a person's perception of events, rather than the events themselves, determine how they feel and act. It is a problem-focused form of treatment that helps a person understand the relationship between beliefs, thoughts, or feelings and the behaviors and actions that result. CBT rests on the theory that behavior and emotions are directly influenced by adjustments in thought patterns.

Through cognitive therapy, a client can reframe negative reactions and learn new, positive emotional and behavioral responses to challenging situations. Problems are often broken down into small manageable parts, and by setting goals the therapist can help the client adjust the way they think, feel, and react.

Cognitive behavioral therapy can be effective for those with clearly defined behavioral and emotional concerns as well as those with specific problems that affect their quality of life. CBT-trained therapists often utilize a problem-solving and goal-oriented approach, which can treat a number of issues including depression, anxiety, PTSD, obsessions, phobias, substance abuse, insomnia, anger management, and more.

Cognitive Processing Therapy (CPT)

A short-term, sequenced version of cognitive behavioral treatment, CPT educates patients about PTSD and the nature of their symptoms.

There are four main parts of CPT. It begins with PTSD symptom education and how this type of treatment helps. Next, CPT focuses on increased awareness of thoughts and feelings. Once you become more aware of your thoughts and feelings, you can be taught to challenge these thoughts. Finally, you learn about changes in your beliefs that happen after experiencing trauma.

CPT can increase a person's ability to challenge distorted thoughts about their trauma. It can also help provide an understanding of unhelpful thinking patterns so healthier ways of thinking can emerge.

Emotional Freedom Techniques/Tapping (EFT)

This technique stems from the principle that the cause of negative emotions such as grief, anger, guilt, trauma, fear, and depression is a disruption to the body's energy system. When blockages are released, the problem feeling is also released and moved through the body. During an EFT session a person focuses on a specific issue or problem while physically tapping on certain points of the body, which is meant to release the energy.

The process starts with a beginning statement of the problem along with a complete acceptance of both the problem and one's self. For example, a person may say something to the effect of, "Even though I have persistent anger I completely accept myself." The statement is said three times while tapping on the side of the hand. While continuing to articulate the fear or problem, the client begins to tap on other points—around the face, chest, and head—until the fear or negative feeling begins to decrease.

Many find EFT an effective way to clear feelings and release limiting beliefs, making room for more positive beliefs and feelings to emerge. Learning EFT also empowers someone to take control of their own emotions, as they can tap on a feeling point any time they wish without the assistance of a clinician.

Eye Movement Desensitization and Reprocessing Therapy (EDMR)

Based on the theory that painful memories remain unprocessed due to a high level of disturbance suffered at the time of the event, Eye Movement Desensitization and Reprocessing Therapy (EMDR) posits that eye movements enhance treatment success through neurological changes that assist in healing and recovery from negative memories.

The client is usually asked to reflect on a stored memory while focusing on an external stimulus—often a finger, small stick, taps, or aural tones—delivered by the therapist. During this time of dual attention, new associations can emerge in the form of an insight, other memories, or new emotions.

EMDR therapy typically focuses on past events, current triggers, and future needs, often in relation to post-traumatic stress. Studies published by *The Journal of EMDR Practice and Research* and *The Journal of Traumatic Stress* show it is possible to alleviate distressing symptoms, particularly those associated with post-traumatic stress, more rapidly with EMDR than with talk therapy alone. Also, because discussing the details of a traumatic experience is not required in EMDR sessions, the anxiety associated with confronting and revealing those details may be alleviated.

Equine- and Animal-Assisted Therapy

Equine- and animal-assisted therapy involves the use of horses or other animals to help with self-awareness and emotional healing. The benefits of the bond between an animal and human are fostered, which elicits nurturing emotions. People frequently respond positively to caring for an animal.

Animal-assisted therapy involves much more than simply spending time with an animal. Usually there are specific therapeutic goals, strategies, and outcome measures. Therapeutic experiences can include walking, brushing, petting, and caring for the animal. Equine therapy does not typically involve riding a horse. Rather, challenging relationships or experiences can be worked through with the support of the animal.

The psychological and physiological benefits of equine- and animal-assisted therapy have been well documented. Improvements in health can include: decreased stress, reduction of anger, improved social interactions, decrease in heart rate and blood pressure, and improved sense of trust and empowerment. A child unable to experience physical and emotional comfort with others may find they are able to freely form that bond with a horse or other animal. Young children in particular can see significant improvements in interpersonal relationships with equine therapy.

Masgutova Neurosensorimotor Reflex Integration℠ (MNRI®)

When we experience trauma, our primary reflexes come into play in order to protect and serve us. PTSD coincides with these primary reflex patterns, remaining in an active state. Individuals may experience various symptoms, such as anxiety, irritability, difficulty sleeping, difficulty focusing, sensitivity to sounds, a decreased immune system, and more. MNRI, also known as the Masgutova Method, addresses primary reflex patterns.

MNRI is a nonverbal, body-based therapy that uses movement and stretches to address the activity in our reflexes in response to stress or trauma. Following an initial assessment, specific reflex challenges are identified and a basic treatment plan is created. Often clients are provided with a simple home program and instruction on how to apply basic MNRI techniques between visits. MNRI is reported to be a calming, relaxing experience for both children and adults.

MNRI targets the emotional center of the brain without talk therapy in a gentle and non-invasive way in order to achieve proper realignment of the sensory-motor reflexes.

Music Therapy

Music therapy integrates music and therapy to help heal mind, body, emotion, and spirit. A trained, board-certified music therapist uses the nonverbal language of music to initiate contact with the client and foster a relationship that can develop a sense of safety for children and adults who have experienced trauma. It can be used to create strategies for stress management, creative expression, communication, social support, positive coping, and resilience.

Working individually or in dyad, family, or group sessions, clients work with music therapists through individualized experiences like song discussion, improvisation, listening, instrument playing, drumming, songwriting, and singing. No previous musical experience is required to participate in and benefit from music therapy. Through musical involvement in the therapeutic context, clients' abilities are strengthened and transferred to other areas of their lives.

Music therapy provides helpful communication avenues to those who struggle to express themselves in words. Research in music therapy supports its effectiveness in helping people who have experienced trauma through increased relaxation, improved self-esteem, decreased anxiety, increased communication, enhanced relationships, better group cohesiveness, and safe emotional release. Because music therapy engages clients on a holistic and creative level, it can elicit responses from those who are unresponsive to traditional therapy.

Neurofeedback and Biofeedback

Neurofeedback and biofeedback supply brain activity feedback in real time to help self-regulation. Specifically, the goal of biofeedback is to take the information gathered from the body's physical responses to stimuli or events and use it to better understand and eventually transform physical and emotional reactions. The goal of neurofeedback is to train brain activity, thereby improving the brain's overall function. Neurofeedback therapy takes abnormal brain patterns and makes them normal. This creates greater flexibility and control to shift from states of arousal to relaxation.

Session begins with an assessment followed by a brain scan that should offer insight into the condition that brought the client in for treatment. Sensors placed on different spots on the client's head measure the activity. Feedback is received through a variety of mediums, including video, audio, imagery, and motion. Information relating to the activity level of the brain at each specific moment is made available through these outlets.

Neurofeedback allows a client to alter their brainwaves and is beneficial for those suffering issues that directly affect brain activity. Neurofeedback training for the mind is similar to physical training for the body. It is a non-invasive technique that prompts the brain to draw from its existing resources to overcome the present condition. Neurofeedback has been shown to improve mood anxiety, depression, ADHD, sleep disorders, and other cognitive impairments that can result from injury. It has also been known to alleviate stress, nausea, migraines, pain, and psychosomatic disorders.

Biofeedback can influence the autonomic nervous system by measuring body functions, such as heart rate, breathing, and muscle tension, allowing the individual to mirror positive connections. It is regularly administered for relaxation training and stress management.

Play Therapy

Through a variety of activities, play therapy utilizes the power of play to transform current life issues. It is a structured, theoretical approach wherein play is the primary tool and language is secondary. Play therapy differs from ordinary play in that the therapist helps children address and resolve their own problems. Play therapy builds on the natural way children learn about themselves and their relationship to the world.

Sessions may be individual or in groups of children. A variety of therapeutic play techniques are used according to the child's age and interests, such as sand trays, dolls, puppets, blocks, bubble blowing, and more.

Through play, the child is given strategies to cope with difficulties they may be powerless to change. It can also provide the therapist with valuable insight into what the child is experiencing, as many children can or will better express their needs and feelings through imagination and play.

Reiki

Reiki is an ancient Japanese stress reduction and relaxation practice known to promote healing. It is based on the idea that the practitioner can share energy with another person—with or without touch—to encourage the natural healing process of the body and mind.

During a Reiki session, the therapist may use light touch or hover their hands above the body. Some may follow a predetermined sequence of placements while others will freely move their hands in no particular order to areas in which they feel energy is most needed.

Reiki is a simple, natural, and safe practice. It can work in conjunction with other medical or therapeutic techniques to relieve physical side effects and promote recovery. When the body is holding the negative energy of a traumatic experience, Reiki is often administered with cognitive therapies to enhance positive energy flow and bring the body back into balance. The negative energy is dispelled or released. Reiki has been integrated into many hospitals for help with pain management, recovery from surgery, and to reduce symptoms of cancer treatment.

Somatic Experiencing

Somatic experiencing (SE), or body-oriented experiencing, makes no distinction between body and mind and encourages "communication" between the two. It is a system often used for relieving trauma symptoms as well as chronic stress. SE offers a framework to assess where a person is "stuck" in the fight-flight-freeze responses, and provides clinical tools to resolve these fixated physiological states. SE teaches that trauma affects the brain, mind, and body, positing that trauma is not caused by the event itself, but rather develops through the failure of the body, psyche, and nervous system to process adverse events.

The main goal of somatic experiencing is recognition and release of physical tension that remains in the body after a traumatic event. Clients are gently guided to develop increased tolerance for difficult bodily sensations and suppressed emotions. Depending on the form of somatic psychology used, sessions may include awareness of bodily sensations, dance, breathing techniques, voice work, physical exercise, movement, and healing touch.

SE does not require that the traumatized person retell or relive the traumatic event. Instead, it offers the opportunity to engage and resolve—

in a slow and supported way—the body's instinctual fight-flight-freeze responses. Individuals locked in anxiety or rage can relax into a growing sense of peace and safety.

Somatic experiencing can initiate bodily sensations that contradict those of fear and helplessness. This resets the nervous system, restores inner balance, enhances resilience to stress, and increases vitality, equanimity, and the capacity to actively engage in life. When somatic experiencing is completed, the patient often reports feeling less stressed and more engaged with life.

Transcranial Magnetic Stimulation (TMS)

Transcranial magnetic stimulation is a procedure that uses magnetic fields to stimulate nerve cells in the brain in order to improve symptoms of depression. Magnetic pulses stimulate nerve cells in the region of the brain involved in mood control. The stimulation affects how this part of the brain works, which in turn can ease depression and improve mood.

TMS does not require sedation with anesthesia and is done on an outpatient basis in a doctor's office. An electromagnetic coil is placed against the scalp near the forehead. The coil creates electric currents that stimulate nerve cells in the region of the brain involved in mood control and depression. It requires a series of sessions to be effective—usually forty-minute sessions carried out five times a week for four to six weeks.

While depression is often treatable, sometimes standard treatments are not effective. TMS can be used when treatments such as medication and talk therapy have been unsuccessful.

Trauma-Focused Cognitive Behavioral Therapy (TF-CBT)

TF-CBT incorporates interventions specifically tailored to meet the needs of adults or children experiencing emotional and psychological difficulties as a result of a trauma and combines them with cognitive behavioral and familial strategies. Individuals learn how to process the emotions and thoughts that relate to the traumatic experience. They are also given tools to alleviate overwhelming thoughts that can cause stress, anxiety, and depression, along with skills to manage emotions in a healthier way.

A secure and stable environment is provided so details of the trauma can be safely disclosed. Cognitive and learning theories of treatment are also applied. Strategies to help cope with and limit perceptions are offered so that the individual can redesign those qualities related to the trauma. With children, parents are also given the resources and skills necessary to help their kids cope with the psychological ramifications of the trauma.

Those suffering severe emotional repercussions due to trauma often respond well to TF-CBT. The therapy can help children who have experienced repeated episodes of trauma, as in abuse or neglect, or those who have suffered one occurrence of sudden trauma in their lives. Children learning to cope with the death of a loved one can also benefit from TF-CBT.

Yoga Therapy

Yoga therapy uses yoga, meditation, and guided imagery to improve physical and emotional health. Trauma-centered yoga therapy specifically supports the process of healing for survivors of trauma and those suffering with PTSD.

Yoga therapy utilizes postures, breathing exercises, and relaxation techniques to suit individual needs. It differs from a yoga class in that tools are integrated and used for therapeutic benefit. Yoga therapy may incorporate postures, such as "downward-facing dog" or "legs up the wall," along with breathing techniques that can also be practiced at home. While trauma involves a lack of choice, trauma-centered yoga therapy asks individuals to make choices around what feels best or most comfortable. Identifying how the body feels can be difficult for trauma survivors. A nurturing environment of choice offers the freedom to try new poses or experiences.

Yoga therapy is used for depression and anxiety. It is also shown to be effective in treatment of PTSD. For trauma survivors, the invitation to choose the poses with which they are most comfortable, as well as how or if they wish to be touched by the therapist, is empowering and can facilitate healing.

RESPONDING TO THE COMMUNITY'S NEEDS THROUGH RECOVERY PROGRAMMING

In addition to connecting individuals and families to the treatment plans that would be most effective for them, we worked to identify and create programs for groups that showed a need for support. Some of these groups were highlighted in the grant, while others surfaced through individual discussions and requests or feedback from surveys and community events.

We believed that group programming should include both education and support. We always tried to create a program that could be sustained beyond our grant term. And because there was a tremendous lack of understanding about the fundamentals of trauma and complicated grief, we tended to incorporate new learning and awareness into our program offerings.

While we reached out for expert assistance in creating quality programming, our knowledge continued to grow. The field of trauma is expansive, and new research seems to provide breakthrough understandings of the complexities of the work all the time. It is important to match programs to the needs presented in your community. You do not need to be the expert, but be willing to seek answers and consult those who are, or bring the experts in if their experience may resonate better with the groups you serve.

The following is a snapshot of the programs we developed.

Local Clinicians

We brought local providers together for an initial meeting to discuss their needs. This event allowed us to register those who were not in our database. The feedback we received allowed us to plan a series of workshops on innovative trauma treatments, such as brainspotting, and new concepts in vicarious traumatization, like trauma stewardship. This concept responds to and creates awareness for the cumulative toll that suffering, hardship, crisis, or trauma can have on individuals and communities. Trauma stewardship fosters discussions about the altering effects of trauma and the strategies to achieve life balance and wellness. The practice is not only relevant to individuals with trauma exposure, it can be applied to organizations, institutions, movements, and communities that have been exposed to suffering, hardship, crisis, or trauma.

We brought in experts in the field to deliver these presentations. Finally, we invited the clinicians to participate in a peer supervision group that continued to meet after our grant term ended.

First Responders

"Recovery for Emergency Responders and Loved Ones" was a yearlong project for which I brought in an organization comprised of former first responders known as HEART 9/11. The group is an expert-led, volunteer-driven, nonprofit disaster-relief organization. Their mission is to rebuild communities and the lives of people coping with disasters and related trauma through contact with veterans of tragedy response—people who have walked the walk. After experiencing initial reluctance from the Newtown first responder community to participate in treatment programs, I partnered with this organization.

HEART 9/11 uniquely matches "volunteer professionals who leverage their unparalleled experience to support, supplement, and transfer skills and knowledge to suffering communities in the same spirit that the world supported New York City after September 11, 2001."

Helping our first responders build resiliency through contact with peers rather than clinical professionals was the key to engaging this group. I worked closely with HEART 9/11 to develop a program that specifically catered to the needs of this community.

Town Employees

This program was a series of lunch meetings to address topics identified through an employee survey we developed. The issues included sleep health, effective fitness, healthy eating, and more. We then created a daylong wellness fair titled "A Passport to Health and Wellness," and had department heads encourage staff to attend. We hired local professionals to provide hands-on demonstrations and treatments in areas such as acupuncture, chiropractic massage, yoga, aromatherapy, tapping, and many more. Those who participated were given a passport to stamp at each station, which they could submit into a raffle for prizes, such as a day off from work.

Sandy Hook School Staff

We developed a daylong retreat for Sandy Hook School staff and their family members to jumpstart their trauma education and programming. We then integrated our trauma specialist into the Sandy Hook Elementary School, where she set up office hours and opened her doors for ongoing support. We also embedded ourselves in planning meetings for continued and future programming. We assisted in bringing important factors to light, including the school staff's need to be a part of any planning process and the importance of creating a safe environment for staff to express their challenges in the classroom and in their personal lives as they related to trauma exposure.

In the rest of the schools, our care coordinators provided support in a collaborative manner. This included education and an introduction to tools and strategies.

Clergy Support

I arranged for a clergy group discussion and education program to explore topics such as how to provide spiritual guidance to those whose faith has been shattered, and how to sustain your work when your community is afflicted by tragedy. We hired Lisa Cataldo, a professor of pastoral counseling at New York University who wrote several articles on these topics, to lead the discussions and provide lessons and support.

Medical Professionals

There was a true partnership between a local pediatric group and our care coordinators. Patients and families that showed signs of distress due to the tragedy were referred to us, and when meeting these individuals, care coordinators discussed the long-term effects of childhood trauma and screening tools available to assist in assessing and predicting risk factors. I created a format to continue this discussion in partnership with the local hospital and its pediatric medicine department. We brought in the Child Health and Development Institute of Connecticut to present an educational program to teach pediatricians the importance of trauma screens in children. The Adverse Childhood Experiences study was highlighted. We invited all local pediatricians and held the workshop during the hospital's grand rounds.

Community Leaders

We hosted a program identified in the DOJ grant as "A Convocation for Educating and Training Leaders." It explained the need for leaders of social services, religious, civic, educational, mental and physical health, and local government organizations to understand the basic concepts of trauma and building resiliency, and how these concepts related to their constituents. We treated this as a formal dialogue with town leaders to review the aftereffects of the tragedy and the best ways to meet the public's needs. I brought in a nationally recognized expert on child grief and community recovery, Ken Druck, PhD, to mediate the workshop, and invited all relevant town department heads and organization directors.

I also created special workshops for school and government heads whenever we offered a new educational program for other groups. An example of this was the trauma stewardship program; a special workshop with that expert was geared toward community leaders, allowing them to be open and vulnerable without exposure to the people they served.

Community at Large

Our team made a concerted effort to be visible at community events such as the Health Fair, Earth Day, the Sandy Hook 5K, Yoga Fest, and others. We also created programs to address certain issues that came to our attention. We collaborated on a wellness education fair. We provided group sessions of emotional freedom tapping for school staff after a lockdown scare and for parents. We provided educational sessions about the use of aromatherapy. We hosted an ongoing support group for families of surviving children who witnessed the shooting.

Finally, we formed collaborative relationships with foundations and organizations like the Parent Connection, Resiliency Center, Ana Grace Project (the Bruce Perry conference), and the Prevention Council. This included attending training and planning meetings for events hosted by established groups working towards recovery, highlighting their efforts on our website, asking for their consultation when addressing relevant concerns, reaching out when raising program funds to meet goals and include their organization. One of the essential elements of building a healthy community after a tragedy is to partner with and support organizations that promote healing. Your efforts can complement theirs.

And the work will have more chance of succeeding if you include those individuals whose efforts laid the foundation for support. Newtown had several organizations doing great work for their community.

IN SUMMARY

When providing a community with recovery resources and programs, you must first identify specific needs and gaps in services, and be prepared to address them at the individual micro-level and the group or community macro-level. Healing treatments need to cover a variety of stages in a person's recovery. Programs should be both educational and supportive. All offerings should be sustainable after your team is gone.

Always assume your audience is not well versed on the effects of trauma. Many groups, such as community leaders, clinicians, and first responders, have their own culture and nuances that may need targeted programming. Treatments are not a one-size-fits-all endeavor; creating individualized plans for recovery and resiliency is important. At the same time, the power of community programming and group support throughout the process is invaluable.

CHAPTER EIGHT

ADDRESSING FAMILIES WHO LOST A LOVED ONE

December 14, 2012 began like any other day in Sandy Hook. Parents kissed their children goodbye and sent them to school with expectations to reunite in a few hours for a gingerbread house-making party, or to see their child's creation when he or she came home from school. Instead, the majority of them would be summoned to pick up their children at a nearby firehouse during a serious crisis. They were alerted—along with the rest of the community—that a deadly shooting had taken place inside the school.

In all, 456 students were enrolled at Sandy Hook Elementary School. Twenty first-graders and six school personnel were killed by troubled local resident Adam Lanza, and the majority of the victims were shot multiple times. Most of the shootings took place in two first-grade classrooms, yet the initial shots were heard throughout the school. Lanza's first victims were the principal and school psychologist, who had been engaged in a morning meeting in the main office. A third teacher was shot and injured in the hallway.

In the first classroom Lanza entered, near the front entrance of the school, a substitute teacher, a behavioral therapist, and fifteen students were shot and killed. One first-grader in the room survived by pretending to be dead. Lanza entered a second classroom and fatally shot the teacher, a teacher's aide, and five more first-grade students. Eleven students in that classroom survived. In the end, the victims included eight boys and twelve girls between the ages of six and seven, and six adults. The shooting took place during morning announcements, and much of it, including the initial gunshots, 911 calls, screaming, and sirens, were heard by the entire school over the public address system.

Every person present at Sandy Hook Elementary School on the morning of December 14, 2012 was impacted. Several teachers hid their students in closets, bathrooms, and under desks until emergency personnel indicated it was safe to unlock their doors. The press called the event "the deadliest mass shooting at either a high school or grade school in US history," a sad distinction it still holds.

FOCUSING ON THE VICTIM FAMILIES

The entire country had its eyes on the victim families in the days and months following the shooting. Newtown was inundated with media; there was a camera lens on every person willing to share their experience. The images and backstories of the children and adults who were killed appeared on every mainstream news outlet. The parents' stories of grief, and questions about how each family was dealing with its unspeakable loss, were also prevalent.

In the weeks following the tragedy, many local and national politicians, including President Barack Obama, personally spoke with the victim families. At the same time, religious masses and vigils were held, along with public outcries for changes to gun laws and mental health protocols. The discussions about potential prevention, responsibility, gaps in the system, and lack of awareness about gun violence became topics of intense interest within the community and on the national news. Many victim families and other Newtown residents became vocal participants in movements for change. Organizations were created with specific advocacy agendas, and the public's response to the crisis seemed to grow.

Some organizations focused on creating awareness and education concerning the need for gun control. There were also those focused on raising money for the victims' recovery. Some became involved in global activism. Others focused on local efforts to address and promote wellness. Research and education initiatives were launched. Some groups invested in service delivery or individual projects. Not surprisingly, divides developed over conflicting viewpoints, which created more drama and tension within the community.

All of this took place at a time when the victim families were at their most vulnerable. After burying their children and loved ones, they had to go through the motions of daily living while continuing to grieve, and navigate their healing needs with cameras still on them.

COMPLICATED GRIEF

Bereavement is an inevitable part of life and can follow several stages that together are a natural response to losing someone you love. Elisabeth Kübler-Ross and David Kessler's definition of the five stages of grief is a popular standard in the realm. These stages are denial, anger, bargaining, depression, and acceptance. Losing someone you love is one of the most difficult experiences a person can endure. But as the pain lessens, we tend to adapt through time and find a way to accept the finality of the loss and move forward in a positive way.

For many families who endure the sudden death of a child or family member in an extreme act of violence like the Sandy Hook shooting, grief follows an atypical trajectory, called *complicated grief*. This type of grief is characterized by more chronic, prolonged, and intense symptoms that persist for more than six months. The symptoms often include preoccupying thoughts of the person who died or the circumstances of the tragedy. This may take the form of images of the victim in their mind or obsession over the final moments of the tragedy. With no outlet for anxiety and anger, a prolonged reaction and preoccupation with details of the event may set in. It's as if the mind tries to find meaning or purpose in the loss and gets stuck in a trauma reel that constantly replays.

Complicated grief can be crushing, and often leaves those who suffer from it with a changed perspective on the world. The traumatic, senseless nature of the death can perpetuate a state of shock, anxiety, and anger. Survivor families often experience an overwhelming intensity of emotions that inhibit the ability to cope with daily tasks. These symptoms can be so intrusive they have an immobilizing effect. Basic functioning may become a constant struggle, as if there can be no positive purpose in life until sense is made of the tragic circumstances of the death.

Someone experiencing complicated grief might avoid any possibility of being triggered by reminders of their loss. This can include avoiding family and friends. As they isolate, they may feel consumed by anger, disillusionment, guilt, and pain. Excessive anxiety and major depression often coincide with these symptoms. Although this intense grief may be acceptable for a period of time, many of those around the individual eventually become weary of the symptoms and find it difficult to be around the person, believing that it's time to move on. Worse, when someone is stuck in their grief, those around them feel helpless. And that is not a state anyone is comfortable in. The result is that the person experiencing complicated grief self-isolates while their friends and family also withdraw.

The following is a formal breakdown of the criteria for complicated grief from the American Psychiatric Association's *Diagnostic and Statistical Manual of Mental Disorders (DSM-5)*. These guidelines may be used as a screening tool to evaluate and treat complicated grief.

At least one of the following symptoms of persistent intense acute grief has been present for six months, or a period longer than is expected by others in the social or cultural environment:

- Persistent intense yearning or longing for the person who died.
- Frequent intense feelings of loneliness, emptiness, or that life is meaningless without the person who died.
- Recurrent thoughts that it is unfair, meaningless, or unbearable to have to live when a loved one has died, or a recurrent urge to die in order to join the deceased.

- Frequent preoccupying thoughts about a person who died; thoughts or images of the person intrude on usual activities or interfere with functioning.

At least two of the following symptoms are present for at least one month:

- Frequent troubling rumination about circumstances or consequences of the death.
- Recurrent feeling of disbelief or inability to accept the death.
- Persistent feeling of being shocked, stunned, dazed, or emotionally numb since the death.
- Recurrent feelings of anger or bitterness related to the death.
- Persistent difficulty trusting or caring about other people, or feeling intensely envious of others who haven't experienced a similar loss.
- Frequently experiencing pain or other symptoms that the deceased person had, hearing the voice, or seeing the deceased.
- Experiencing intense emotional or physiological reactivity to memories of the person who died.
- Change in behavior due to excessive avoidance, or the opposite, excessive proximity seeking, i.e. refraining from going places, doing things or having contact with things that are a reminder of the loss, or feeling drawn to reminders of the person such as wanting to see, touch, hear, or smell things to feel close to the deceased.

The grief process for shooting victim families is very different from that of a loss that did not occur suddenly or in the context of a traumatic event. The post-traumatic stress and pervasive grief often results in a loss of self; when your world has been shattered, you feel exposed, vulnerable, and consumed by distressing thoughts and emotions related to the death. Most family members will never return to a life that does not include this sense of vulnerability or lack of control.

Remember, these parents or siblings thought that school day was going to be another normal day. They expected their children to come home as they had the day before. When the reality hits that your loved one is not coming home, time seems to stop. The safe world you once knew becomes a fantasy. Familiar surroundings are now filled with constant reminders of the family member's presence—a life that is now gone. But stepping out of familiar surroundings can also frighten and confuse—the world is full of reminders of what occurred, even when you want to pretend the event never happened.

Adults feeling the burden of complicated grief may also believe they have to move on to support other family members. So you go on, but with a pervasive sense of despair, anger, and confusion about why everything feels unreal and different. While we know the most important thing for those grieving is to take care of themselves and surviving family members, the overwhelming need to make sense of the tragedy can supersede the ability to focus on self-care. This is why it is particularly important to create a safe, respectful environment for these families to heal in that includes the provision of services to cover basic needs.

It is natural for humans to want answers to life events. We believe there will be comfort in knowing or understanding the rationale behind events that occur outside our control. But for those experiencing complicated grief, I am not sure there is comfort even when there are answers. The loss is too unfathomably difficult. But that doesn't halt the desperate urge to know what happened and why. As a consequence, many individuals who experience loss through violence and aggression express a shattering of the faith or religious beliefs that once kept them grounded. They may no longer take comfort in faith because their loss seems so unfair.

The presence of the media, and images of the tragedy replaying on television, can also trigger feelings of helplessness and pain, making closure from complicated grief particularly difficult to achieve. These images may unexpectedly reactivate unresolved thoughts of what the last moments of life may have been like for those who died. In Newtown we heard the phrase "we want to respect the family's privacy" often, when in fact the victim families were consistently bombarded with devastating footage from which there was no privacy. Some families took comfort in talking about their loss, some felt the need to isolate, and many found the fishbowl-like atmosphere unwelcoming and became skeptical of the media's intent. Eventually, after numerous families expressed that they were struggling with the notoriety, the town organized a pushback to protect their privacy. In news conferences for the one-year anniversary, it was requested that the media have a restrained presence and that the public respect the privacy of victim families, focusing instead on acts of kindness and volunteer work for charitable organizations. The state legislature also passed a bill to restrict access to autopsy reports, death certificates, and graphic photos of the victims.

The media coverage had allowed for a massive outpouring of empathy and support from around the world, with thousands of letters and items sent to the town for the victim families. But some said that while the donations, gifts, written posts, articles, and artwork were appreciated, the sheer number and constant influx of them felt re-traumatizing.

What's more, when tragedy occurs in a community where neighbors' lives are intertwined, more than just the victim families feel that grief. And this pervasiveness can negatively impact the victim families as well. For some Sandy Hook parents, simple tasks like going to the grocery store or coffee shop became unmanageable. They would wander down aisles in a numb state, struggling with simple choices, and could feel the looks of helplessness and pain on the faces of people who realized that they were in the company of a parent whose child was killed.

EFFECTIVE WAYS TO SUPPORT VICTIM FAMILIES

In the days following the shooting, each family was assigned a state police officer to escort them to meetings and events and to provide protection from the outside world. As individual families' needs were assessed, federal, state, and local supports included financial assistance, relocation help, educational assistance for surviving children, and clinical and community-based mental health services. The NRRT entered the scene a year and a half after the shooting, and by this time, many of the most impacted families had built strong support networks and were receiving excellent mental health treatment. Funds were distributed directly to these families to ease costs of therapy and other expenses related to the tragedy, and trusts were set up with the Connecticut Office of Victim Services for future expenses. Great thought and care went into these decisions. Yet there were still dissenting opinions about whether the distribution amounts were adequate. The weight of this decision must have been heavy. No amount of money given to a family that lost a child will feel adequate or fair. Weighing this decision against the potential needs of the community at large is also an impossible task. I cannot assess whether these decisions were adequate for those impacted, but they were certainly made with the best intentions. Financial limits had to be set.

In the immediate aftermath of the tragedy, prior to the NRRT's inception, one Newtown resident formed a unique and supportive network, called My Sandy Hook Family, to assist and protect these families. This included an organized system to address immediate, emotional, and financial needs. A network of volunteers assembled to provide rides to pick up family members at the airport before the funerals or help with daily tasks like snow removal, preparing and delivering meals, house cleaning, childcare, making sure bills were paid, and other neighborly services. They launched a private website that only victim families could access. This website also acted as a tool to privately request services and support and as a means for families to communicate amongst each other. This proved to be a very effective means for families to connect without exposure to outsiders. The site was well protected by its participants, who said it was the only way they could ensure their personal experiences would not be exploited and that fellow victim family members could reach out with ease.

The grant that defined the scope of our services stated that we were to address the needs of the community at large, but it became immediately clear that we had to address those most impacted as a distinct group with unique needs and concerns. We set about our work believing that it would take time to build trust and rapport with these families. We had to prove we were professionals who could benefit them before being accepted.

Even after our office was established, some individuals and families continued to seek clinical support from outside sources. I believe that two years out, most families had secured their support network and were adjusting to a "new normal." Some said that they did not want to sit with yet another expert or hear one more perspective on grief and healing. We honored that and chose to include the families in all our events if they wished to participate. We asked for input and suggestions on what might help them. We offered private individual and group time with any presenter we brought to Newtown. There was not a lot of interest. This was an indication of where everyone was in his or her healing journey.

They received notifications of our service offerings along with the rest of the community, but I did my best to honor their need for privacy. I used a special sensitivity when inviting victim families to participate in recovery efforts with the broader community, and sent letters to each head of household and/or adult family member introducing myself and the team and outlining our mission and responsibilities. I highlighted our strict ethics and confidentiality policies, including that all consultations would be private and each individual would be assigned an advocate and care coordinator who would stay with them for the duration of our recovery work. I also offered to meet with any individual or group at their support network meetings to answer questions, and made it clear I was available to discuss flexibility with services, if they felt that was warranted.

To my surprise, I did not hear from any of the victim families after my letter went out. The only response came several months later at an event we hosted. A mother who had lost her child told me that I should have worked harder to reach out to the group. When I asked if she had received my letter, she responded, "Oh, I ripped it up and threw it away without reading it. As soon as I saw the return address of Newtown Recovery and Resiliency Team, I was so angry that there was yet another thing that existed because my child is gone, I didn't want to look at it."

Following this response, we made sure our communications were delivered in multiple formats, including email, Facebook, marketing flyers, our website, the local newspaper, other foundation websites, and banners. I made several attempts to get invited to the victim families support network meetings to present our services and discuss their needs. Even then, the group was slow to engage. However, over time, several individuals and families from this victim group did reach out to us.

We continued to be thoughtful and sensitive to the journey they were on. Eventually, we took calls for appointments with our care coordinators. A few parents walked into our office with immediate needs. We provided valuable resources, including assistance navigating their health insurance, the OVS trust, and other funding realms. We advocated for items that didn't fall into the established guidelines for financial assistance, including funeral costs and summer camp for a victim's sibling.

I mention these details not to paint a picture of resistance, but to illustrate the challenge of engaging those who are highly traumatized and grief-stricken. There was no ill intent on their part, just weariness. One individual said to me months later, "Please, no more experts." As I stated before, because of our timing, some of their supports had already been well established, and decisions as to who was trustworthy had already been made.

My lack of awareness for the magnitude of their anguish contributed to a less than optimal ability to engage these families from the outset.

However, as I worked with them I began to realize how important it was to individualize the healing process. Every family was different in its level of grief, supports, and awareness of the ways trauma had impacted their lives. Some families stayed silent, some were outspoken, and most only sought assistance once a level of trust was established. Some families told us they only felt comfortable working with a familiar face, and others aired concerns about disclosing information to people within the broader community. Some families wished to receive information by phone, others by email, some by traditional mail, some in person, and others not at all.

Our goal was to make sure their voices were heard and their needs were met to the best of our ability. This required us to find a successful means of engagement. I came to understand that this would be an exercise in patience and flexibility. We did not want to disappoint them. We did not want to appear inaccessible or unfocused on their needs. However, I underestimated how guarded the families would be. Looking back, it is easy to understand why they did not embrace our presence with ease. To many we represented a group born out of their tragic loss, and may not have appeared value added. It took multiple outreach attempts before comfortable connections were made. We had to determine how we could be of value to them.

I also developed a new familiarity with the face of trauma and complicated grief. I accepted being treated to feelings of appreciation one day and frustration the next—expressions that came from a place of emotional dysregulation. Everyone on my team had to be comfortable with the level of pain these individuals were experiencing and know that even on a good day, someone may be triggered into a more aggressive or vulnerable response to their loss. A top priority became respecting emotional vulnerability with complete confidentiality while delivering the help and services that these individuals needed.

The families took many roads after their loss. Some chose to move. There were those who stayed in town and formed foundations to memorialize their loved ones. Some became strong advocates for mental health reform and/or gun violence prevention. Some families took legal action. A campaign for school safety was launched by others. Some took public platforms while others coveted privacy. Our challenge was to quietly establish a community presence alongside the great work of these families. Many were light years ahead of us in the quest to move forward and seek resilience in the wake of unspeakable loss. So many lessons could be taken from their examples of turning tragedy into a forum for education, awareness, and change.

The following is a snapshot of victim family efforts to honor a loved one lost on 12/14:

- Charlotte Bacon's family supports a therapy dog program, a scholarship for students studying to become veterinarians, and a grant to help couples grieving the death of a child. Her parents co-wrote a children's book, *Good Dogs, Great Listeners,* which tells the story of Charlotte's love for her dog Lily. Charlotte's brother also wrote a book about his experience with therapy dogs after his sister's death.
- Daniel Barden's family launched a kindness campaign, "What Would Daniel Do?" in his honor. His father is a member of the Sandy Hook Promise, a nonprofit

organization that advocates for mental health reform, stronger gun laws, and violence prevention.

The organization has developed educational programs and a successful media presence to alert the public to signs that someone is at risk of using violence. His parents participated in a lawsuit against gun manufacturers over their irresponsible advertising campaigns.

- Olivia Engel's family has raised funds for Zest For Life, which supports the Newtown "Park and Bark" group. A website in Olivia's honor highlights pictures of her and her love for dogs, soccer, swimming, dancing, and singing, among other things.

- Ana Grace Marquez-Greene's family created the Ana Grace Project. It supports two platforms: arts education that integrates a "Love Wins" curriculum to promote a stronger social and emotional environment for students and educators, and professional development for trauma-informed care and counseling for all communities. Her father, a prominent jazz musician, released an album in 2014, *Beautiful Life,* as a tribute to his daughter. Her mother participates in forums to bring awareness to grief and the survivor's perspective on community violence.

- Dylan Hockley's parents formed the foundation Wings Of Change, which benefits children with autism and other special needs. His mother is an active member of Sandy Hook Promise and a prominent speaker on gun violence prevention and mental health awareness. She has participated in legal action against gun manufacturers, distributors, and dealers of military-style weapons.

- Catherine Hubbard's family built an animal sanctuary to honor her. The sanctuary hosts events and raises funds to support its operations.

- Chase Kowalski's family formed the CMAK Foundation in honor of him. The fund supports programs that promote the physical and emotional well-being of children, including a triathlon for kids.

- Jesse Lewis' family formed the Jesse Lewis Choose Love Movement in his honor. It offers a downloadable social and emotional learning program for teachers and students, as well as scholarships. Jesse's mother has spoken and written about her experiences and the importance of integrating kindness and social awareness into learning. Jesse's brother has become involved in a reciprocal healing partnership with survivors of the Rwandan genocide.

- James Mattioli's family created the James R. Mattioli Memorial Fund c/o Newtown Savings Bank.

- Grace McDonnell's family created the Grace McDonnell Memorial Fund in her honor. It supports young artists and youth art programs.

- Emily Parker's family honored her through the Emily Parker Art Connection. The foundation supports art programs. Her mother wrote a book, *Unseen Angel,* about a spiritual path to coping, healing, and forgiving in the wake of tragedy. She is also a co-founder of Safe and

Sound Schools, which supports crisis prevention, response, and recovery in schools.

- Noah Pozner's parents work to stop the activities of hoaxers and conspiracy theorists. His father founded the HONR Network, which coordinates volunteers to monitor and respond to hoaxer posts and videos. HONR also helps grieving families deal with online abuse and lobbies social media companies to stop hosting such activity.

- Caroline Previdi's family created the Caroline Previdi Foundation in her honor to provide financial resources for children to engage in their favorite extra-curricular activities.

- Jessica Rekos's family created the Jessica Rekos Foundation. It provides scholarships for horseback riding and supports orca whale research and conversation.

- Avielle Richman's family created The Avielle Foundation. It supports neuroscience research on the brain functions that lead to violence and compassion. The organization also engages in community education programs to create awareness for its findings and promote mental health.

- Benjamin Wheeler's family founded Ben's Lighthouse. The organization offers long-term support to local youth dealing with the aftermath of the Sandy Hook tragedy.

- Allison Wyatt's family honored her through the Allison Wyatt Memorial Foundation. The foundation raises money for St. Jude Children's Research Hospital, Ronald

McDonald House Charities, and the International Child
Art Foundation.

- Rachel Davino, the school's behavioral therapist, was
honored by her family through fundraising activities for
Autism Speaks.

- The family of Dawn Hochsprung, the school principal,
has committed to advocate for gun violence prevention.
Her daughter, Erica Lafferty, has joined Everytown for
Gun Safety and makes frequent media appearances to
speak about her mother and call for stricter gun laws.

- Schoolteacher Lauren Rousseau's family created
scholarships for future educators in her honor at two
schools, Danbury High School and the University of
Bridgeport Graduate School.

- Mary Sherlach's family created Mary's Fund in honor
of the school psychologist. The fund provides access to
mental health care for Connecticut residents who cannot
otherwise obtain it. Mary's husband is a member of the
Sandy Hook Promise and speaks out against gun violence
and assault rifle manufacturers.

- Schoolteacher Victoria Soto's family honored her through
the Victoria Soto Memorial, which provides scholarships
to future teachers and sponsors educational initiatives that
advocate for stricter gun control and gun violence awareness.

TREATMENT PROTOCOLS WHEN
COMPLICATED GRIEF OCCURS WITH TRAUMA

When trauma occurs without the loss of a loved one, it typically includes a period of assessing the perceived threat and its potential implications. Trauma changes your perception of the world, and feelings of anxiety and danger can occur. PTSD may be present. If it is, an individual may have intrusive thoughts and images. They may avoid situations considered threatening. Physiological dysregulation can occur.

To further complicate matters, trauma and complicated grief can co-occur. While the trauma is often confined to the time and space of the event, complicated grief is marked by the feeling that the loss is never over. A persistent sadness and yearning can occur alongside the fear and anxiety that are prominent in the trauma response. Both are distressing and may manifest into risk factors such as suicidal ideation, self-destructive behavior, debilitating anxiety, and depression.

When trauma and complicated grief co-occur, which we know was the case for many in Sandy Hook, the most effective approach to the healing process is a combination of interpersonal, cognitive, and intuitive strategies. Often my staff would recommend layering strategies together simultaneously or in phases. The reason was that when trauma and complicated grief are in play, it's as if both the right and left hemispheres of the brain are under assault. Each side interprets and processes experiences differently. The left brain remembers words, facts, and concrete details; it's our logical side, responsible for organization and translating experiences into words. The right brain stores sensory memories of sound, touch, smell, and the emotions that coincide with these senses. The right brain responds to voices, facial expressions, and body language. In the case of someone who experiences complicated grief, it's as if they have become stuck and cannot integrate new life experiences. The symptoms take on a life of their own for prolonged periods of time, and risk factors can increase. When there is a triggering incident, a traumatized right brain may react as if the memory of the event is happening in the present. This is a classic symptom of PTSD. If the left brain is impaired, the person may express extreme emotions to situations where an extreme reaction is not warranted.

When working in an environment where complicated grief may be prevalent, it is important to understand what you are dealing with, learn how to recognize symptoms, and deliver appropriate resources. You will not be able to engage with impacted individuals effectively and decrease their distress if you cannot identify their particular stress responses, triggers to the trauma memory, or their stuck pattern because of complicated grief. Helping individuals understand and make sense of their experience and symptoms is key to moving forward. Putting an end to any notion that they "should feel better by now" or "will never be able to function normally again" or that "no one will ever understand how hard it is" can be an extremely valuable gift.

We saw tremendous relief in the eyes of a grieving family member when we asked questions related to emotional and physiological symptoms. Next, we set about prescribing the right treatments and strategies while securing a support network. We understood the need for patience and time in the healing process. We followed up with each person who sought our assistance, and kept an open-door policy for moments when they felt re-triggered by an anniversary event, the sound of an ambulance, a news article, or disappointment in the results of a policy campaign. We stepped in to assist with logistics when, for example, individuals lacked a capacity to organize an event or manage insurance claims. We reworked a treatment plan and advocated for services as many times as was necessary for an individual to express relief and move forward without our help.

On the second anniversary of the shooting, there was a divide in the community about how to approach the day. Town leaders wanted to err on the side of business as usual. Yet we heard directly from many who thought there should be vigils and school closings. My team decided to quietly provide resources to those who needed them. I invited Ken Druck, PhD, to an open forum where any impacted family could meet with him in a small group or private meeting. We chose to have Dr. Druck lead this effort because he had addressed the victim families on prior occasions, and has expertise in community grief.

IN SUMMARY

The Newtown community came together to support each other in numerous ways. Many of the families that lost someone gathered on their own for companionship and support through their difficult healing process. Much was done in private. The strength and support of the community occurred naturally before our team came onto the scene. Many individuals had worked tirelessly to create a sense of unity in healing through events that included road races, concerts, vigils, meetings, workshops, memorials, political activism, and other gatherings.

Some found solace creating activities to honor those who died. This may have been through a foundation and its cause, rallying around a political goal, or participating in a spiritual event. Learning to grieve with others is an important step in the healing process.

When we began our work, the community needed help to build and strengthen the clinical and intuitive resources that would address the lingering trauma and complicated grief. Our team researched specific treatments and providers. With a fundamental understanding of what each individual was experiencing, we were able to build rapport and a safe space to provide guidance and assist in building a successful treatment plan.

CHAPTER NINE

SURVIVORS IMPACTED ON SITE:
Teachers, School Personnel, and Students

On the evening of December 14, 2012, US Secretary of Education Arne Duncan issued a statement in appreciation of Sandy Hook School personnel. "Our thanks go out to every teacher, staff member and first responder who cared for, comforted, and protected children from harm, often at risk to themselves," he said. "We will do everything in our power to assist and support the healing and recovery in Newtown."

There were many heroes that day. The principal who alerted others to the shooter's presence and became his first victim, the staff members who helped students hide, and the custodian who ran through the halls locking classroom doors as the massacre occurred. Although the term "first responder" traditionally refers to law enforcement and emergency medical services, SHS staff also acted as first responders during the shooting.

Staff had a responsibility to see students to safety without even knowing the scope of the situation. Teachers made instantaneous decisions to shield students, follow the lockdown protocol, and keep everyone calm, all while feeling terrified over the violent threat lurking in the building. Some hid with students in closets or bathrooms. They read stories or sang songs. Minutes felt like hours as they waited for word that it was safe to come out.

Over the next few hours, as the shooting's magnitude came to light, word got out that the casualties included children and colleagues. While some impacted individuals sought treatment immediately, others stayed home out of fear and confusion. Innocence and lightheartedness disappeared. Many watched the wall-to-wall media coverage to piece together details from the surreal scene they had just witnessed firsthand, though others could not bear to turn on the news. A few teachers appeared in media coverage before they could make sense of what had occurred. Bringing attention to the tragedy feels like a responsibility, but the timing of that disclosure can be the difference between causing more damage and promoting healing.

Many staff attended funerals and participated in vigils and memorials for friends, colleagues, and children they had taught or interacted with. Amplified sounds of gunfire on the loudspeaker, and cries of parents as survivors finally exited the building, kept replaying in their heads. Overwhelming feelings of disbelief, fear, and guilt were even harder to manage in light of public desire to hear their stories, demands to be present for their families in the holiday season, and the need to return to work.

The tragedy displaced them to an empty school in a neighboring town, where they had to set up classrooms and adjust to a new building and principal. They were expected to manage their own wounds while taking care of students who were also traumatized. The shooting occurred right before the winter break, and classes resumed three weeks later. Sandy Hook Elementary School remained a crime scene, but at the new location, resources and guidance were promised. New leadership was arranged since their principal had been killed. Staff was given the option to be placed with different students or at another school. The majority of the teachers and staff initially returned to the temporary school with a commitment to be strong and brave, and resume their responsibility to educate the more than 400 students dealing with the aftermath of the tragedy.

For these teachers, many sights and sounds served as near-constant triggers for intense memories and/or emotions. Later on, several of them told us, "There was life before 12/14 and there was life after 12/14. Nothing will ever be the same." What they were dealing with was a memory bank full of vivid terror, combined with heartbreak as raw as an open wound. These survivors felt unsettled—unable to wrap their heads around what had happened—asking themselves questions like "how?" and "why?" No matter how hard they tried to resume their old lives, an inability to regain their sense of grounding persisted.

As a result, questions lingered as to how the school should address behaviors that would never have received attention before. Discussions about holiday celebrations caused intense emotion and opinion. When a teacher seemed to be having a difficult day, colleagues wondered whether to approach them and offer support, or to stay in the wings, waiting for the individual to reach out.

Within the next few years, 40 percent of the staff left this school for another or retired.

THE NRRT'S ROLE IN SCHOOL STAFF RECOVERY

As I built our recovery and resiliency team and set about identifying individual and group needs, the school's staff and children were obviously among those who needed support. Many staff exhibited sleep disturbances, anxiety, hypervigilance, dissociation, and depression. Indicative of post-traumatic stress, many felt a pervasive loss of safety as a result of having been trapped. Remember, while they listened to the initial shots, warnings, and cries for help, they were unable to communicate with anyone beyond their classrooms to understand the true impact and magnitude of the event. Being locked in time, closed off from the outside world, and unable to receive information about the chaos erupting around them was utterly haunting.

When the Newtown Recovery and Resiliency Team first took shape, town leadership told us that the surviving Sandy Hook Elementary School staff and students had their needs adequately covered with funds from the federal Department of Education's School Emergency Response to Violence (SERV) grant, so we didn't engage. SERV money funded counseling at all the public schools, and their counselors provided trauma-informed resources and in-service workshops to students and staff. The SERV funds supported schools in other ways too. A pool of substitute staff was created and made available for respite when needed. New teachers were hired to fill vacancies. Significant care was taken with security measures, including a police presence at all the schools. The superintendent consistently fielded concerns and solved problems to alleviate stress and anxiety.

So, knowing that SHS staff was not in our domain and the SERV grant was addressing all needs, we focused our efforts on the students and their parents. Yet as the months went by, and as we embedded ourselves in community recovery work, our care coordinators started receiving calls for assistance from SHS staff. We treated these requests like any other— — we opened cases, put individual treatment plans together, and followed up with continued support. As we developed a rapport with them, we heard more stories of staff who felt in need of education and support concerning trauma-related symptoms. Some teachers urged us to reach out to colleagues who were suffering but felt reluctant to come forward.

This prompted me to contact the new school principal, the SERV grant liaison, and a local clinician who was in place to work with SHS staff. I was met with some resistance at first; the general feeling, again, was that adequate resources were in place and everyone's needs were being taken care of. School was functioning, teachers were teaching, and the days of focusing on recovery were lessening. The principal and staff clinician said they had an open-door policy and were able to address any ongoing needs sufficiently. So I let them know I was available if that changed and moved on with my other responsibilities.

A few months later a teacher called our office asking for help finding a legal advocate to provide guidance to a group of teachers on getting their recovery needs met. I brought this information to the appropriate leaders in an NRRT board meeting and received the green light to put together a proposal to develop a recovery response program.

We started by organizing an all-staff meeting for Sandy Hook School personnel, specifically for creating recovery programming. The counselor designated for school staff, the new principal, the assistant principal, the district superintendent, the liaison for the SERV grant, the NRRT trauma specialist, and myself were all in attendance. This turned out to be an emotional meeting. The personnel asked why we focused on other groups and not them. They reminded us that they were the initial first responders on the scene, yet somehow efforts to provide them support didn't match the challenges they still faced. We heard stories of courage, pain, and overwhelming anxiety. We learned about the struggles many had just getting through each day. Accounts of PTSD symptoms included regular triggering responses to sounds and sights, overthinking their decisions and abilities, wondering when they experienced a behavioral issue with a student if it was due to residual trauma, and the sheer emotion that came with any mention of 12/14. Holiday celebrations, birthday celebrations, or hearing about someone's illness or family crisis could all trigger reactions. Going outside, attending field trips, or hosting group events felt unsafe for some. Several teachers said, "We don't know how to teach traumatized kids. And when we ask for guidance we get the same response: 'You're a good teacher. You know what you are doing. Just keep doing what you know.' But this feedback doesn't feel right. Nothing is the same."

Since all the decision-makers were at this meeting, we were able to develop an immediate plan to address these concerns and needs. I put in place on-site access to therapy with our trauma expert twice a week in the temporary school. We would create a one-day retreat for all staff and their significant others to jump-start dialogue about trauma and its impact. The SERV grant liaison worked with the principal to form a committee of administrators, clinicians, school personnel, and the NRRT to craft a yearlong educational and support program to address trauma and grief. The programs in this initiative were hands-on and experiential. Together, these decisions helped create an open, honest dialogue between the principal, grant liaison, our trauma specialist, and myself. We decided that moving forward, school personnel would be included in assessing and planning meetings.

THE TEACHER'S RETREAT

As we neared the end of the school year, I was given a date to hold the retreat and just three weeks to plan it. I preferred to make it a two- to three-day event, but was constrained by classroom and staff family needs. We reached out to the American Counseling Association for advice. Its president identified a talented group of graduate students from the University of Texas who were doing innovative work in the areas of trauma and mind-body connections. I also invited a former teacher from Pennsylvania, Kim Preske, who had survived two fatal school violence incidents. Kim had left teaching to spread awareness and support to other educators.

Over several conference calls we developed an agenda for the retreat. Our mission was to break down misconceptions educators and staff may have had about their ongoing experiences, as well as create deeper connections between them. I insisted that we run the retreat away from Newtown. We rented space in a beautiful hotel and conference facility in a neighboring town. We provided transportation, child care, snacks, and take-home bags with mindfulness items, such as samples of essential oils and audio recordings of meditation and grounding strategies.

There was no money in my budget for this retreat, so I had to fundraise for the program. I reached out to the Sandy Hook Elementary School's parent teacher association. They had offered money to support recovery efforts before, and graciously covered the expense.

The day proved to be a bonding experience and a true jump-start to emotional recovery on a level that these "first responders" had not experienced before. The participants shared their thoughts and feelings both as individuals and as a collective group. They expressed gratitude for the new knowledge and support. They cried and laughed together while expressing fears and setbacks, as well as strategies and successes. There were many aha moments as they listened to the facilitators and practiced exercises in self-regulation and self-care. We held several mini-workshops, all of which were experiential. There was a combination of large and small group activities. We included family members later in the day, in group activities tailored to their needs. At the culmination of the retreat, we all came together for a meal and a few moments to relax and continue nurturing connections.

Following the retreat, we continued to provide therapy and support in the school. We participated in future recovery effort planning for school personnel, forging a comprehensive plan for the following school year. The relationship they built with our team, but particularly with our trauma expert, resulted in many SHS staff members securing helpful treatment for themselves and their families. Several monumental events took place during the next school year that required extra support, and we were able to help provide it. One such event was the transition to the new Sandy Hook Elementary School.

Throughout our tenure, we had the opportunity to listen to these individuals and were able, also, to teach them a few lessons on what trauma looks like and how to make self-care a priority. When we stepped away, we felt like we had played a small role in empowering these "first responders," and we hoped it would last for many years to come.

In the end, they taught us many lessons in resiliency too. Despite their pain and suffering, they showed up to work every day and did a tremendous job educating children who were impacted by a devastating tragedy. They refused to let the shooter shatter their school. They honored those who were lost, including beloved colleagues, and demonstrated true loyalty to the community. They advocated for each other as they found themselves part of a group they would never have wished to join. Some became activists and formed the organization Sandy Hook School Educators for Gun Sense. They wrote books and articles for newspapers and magazines, told their stories in documentaries, and were interviewed on television. But most importantly, they went home every day and continued to care for their friends and families.

TRANSITIONING INTO A NEW SCHOOL BUILDING

The town government, through an extremely intensive process, voted to demolish the original Sandy Hook Elementary School and construct a new building on the same property. The front of the school would not include the area that housed the classrooms where the shooting occurred.

During the last few months of the NRRT mandate, construction for the new Sandy Hook Elementary School began, and the reality that students and staff would have to return to this location set in. Although the architectural design was made with sensitivity, and care was taken to be meaningful in every aspect of the project, for some it still resurrected distress. A re-traumatization effect occurred for many school staff and parents. Signs of dysregulation resurfaced for some. They expressed conflicted thoughts and feelings about the new school and their ability to return there.

Our team was called into the meetings with staff. In one instance, a private tour for the educators during the construction phase, our trauma specialist was in attendance to provide support. It opened with a question many thought they had moved past: "Can I return to teach here?" Once again, feelings of anxiety, guilt, fear, and confusion came up. We helped foster a sense of community among school personnel, and ultimately a safe environment for each person to explore and honor their needs.

The NRRT left Newtown in March 2016, and the new school opened the following September. Our trauma specialist was hired to be at the school one day a week to provide continued support through the transition. Even though there was much concern about reentering the building, most families and personnel did attend the fall opening.

SURVIVOR WITNESS CHILDREN AND THEIR FAMILIES

"Survivor witness children" was how we classified the Sandy Hook students who were in rooms where teachers and classmates did not survive. They exited a bloody scene, walking past twisted bodies and shattered glass, having witnessed murder from just inches away. The children exhibited the expected signs of trauma—nightmares, behavior changes, some triggering when exposed to certain sounds—and their parents were in a state of shock and fear regarding long-term consequences. Most of the children did not have the vocabulary to discuss what they had witnessed or explain its impact on their mental and physical health. However, the children were asking "why?" Some wondered about friends who were killed, others worried that it could happen again. Many children and parents struggled to regain a sense of safety.

This group also had unique concerns. For instance, lots of outside, interested parties wanted to hear from these parents and children, including documentarians, reporters, federal representatives, and others. The conventional wisdom was that children who survived such a horrific event had unique stories to tell. There were many who were interested in hearing these accounts. Fortunately, the parents received valuable guidance early on from two highly trained, trauma-informed clinicians who warned that there might be negative mental health impacts on the surviving child as well as the entire family if they participated in media interviews so soon. The parents also realized that it was important to avoid situations in which the media's agenda wasn't clear or value added. Consequently, very few survivor families responded directly to the press. They did their best to shield their identities and struggles, and as a whole the group kept its exposure to a minimum.

These parents felt grateful that their child had survived, but will forever wonder about impacts that have not been fully presented. Research indicates that children exposed to trauma have a greater risk of developing medical conditions such as heart disease and diabetes. The Adverse Childhood Experiences Study, conducted by Kaiser Permanente and the Centers for Disease Control and Prevention, suggests that children exposed to trauma have a higher rate of developing emotional and/or clinical diagnosis later in life. We heard questions that included:

- Would symptoms manifest next month, next year, or in five years?
- Will my child be more susceptible to stress, mental illness, or disease?

- When my child says she has a stomachache, is that related to the trauma?

- My child cries out in his sleep, shaking. How do I let him know he's safe?

- When my child struggles in school, is it purely academic, or is there an emotional component?

- How do I stay strong and convey a sense of safety and security to my children when I wonder if they will ever be truly safe again?

- Can I relax since my child seems to be adjusting well, or should I worry that the emotional impact has yet to rear its head?

Little research was available on children this age (between six and seven years old) and their long-term impact after similar trauma events. No clear answers were available about what their futures might look like. Other school shootings, like the one in Columbine High School in Littleton, Colorado, involved older students who could more clearly articulate their thoughts and feelings. What we did know was that the shooter stole an innate sense of innocence and safety from these children. He also robbed their parents of the ability to confidently protect and safeguard their children against harm.

Then there was a pervasive sense of guilt. The shooting occurred in a contained room where bullets hit at random. Parents of survivors had the challenge of facing those whose children did not make it home. These thoughts and experiences closely resembled the symptoms of survivor's guilt, but had the added dynamic of fear with memories frozen in time from PTSD. So these parents needed to learn not only about the typical stages of grief—denial, anger, bargaining, depression, and acceptance—but also the signs and symptoms of trauma.

By the time the NRRT was established, parents of these children had already formed a tight-knit support group led by my team's trauma specialist and another licensed professional counselor who resided in town. They had been meeting regularly to share their experiences and show support for each other. They learned about resources and treatments for their children, themselves, and siblings who were struggling. They were able to share their children's stories in a private setting and decide collectively how to proceed with recovery efforts, while carefully evaluating the potential for exposure that could damage their families. While not every family attended the support groups, the majority did, and expressed that they received tremendous comfort in participating. Later, when the formal NRRT took shape, we invited this group to move its meetings to our center. This allowed them direct access to our resources and a familiarity with the extended services we offered.

The families learned that staying close to each other while navigating the school and greater Sandy Hook community was key to their resilience. Building a support system out of a trusting, safe, small community of individuals with similar feelings is a natural resource for healing. Having trained professionals on hand to address their emotional needs made a huge difference as well.

The counselors and group facilitators knew it was important to work at the pace the group was comfortable with. The counselors became advocates, voiced their concerns at public meetings, and eventually introduced strategies and techniques to combat some of the expressed symptoms of trauma into their group sessions. For instance, following discussions about a child having difficulty sleeping, or displaying dysregulated behaviors, they demonstrated grounding techniques such as the use of tapping, aromatherapy, guided imagery, and other mindfulness practices. These techniques are particularly useful to reorient an individual when staying present in the here and now is difficult. They presented effective ways to open a dialogue with children about painful memories or feelings that could help deal with anxiety or episodes of dissociation.

This group of families became a model of support for others to emulate. They discussed requests to participate in events or media presentations with each other and often reached a consensus about which opportunities seemed positive and which might open them or their children up to negativity and potentially damaging exposure. They celebrated milestones and mourned anniversary events together. They formed a cohesive, nurturing, and protective bond. Because of this commitment to emotional health and wellness, it seemed that their children, the witnesses, were healing.

One parent expressed a sentiment shared by everyone in this group: "Not a day goes by that we aren't grateful that our child survived. And not a day goes by that we don't think about the twenty children who did not survive."

IN SUMMARY

There is no denying that the children who witnessed the murder of friends and teachers will be impacted for the rest of their lives. And though they are grateful, the parents of those children will always worry about emotional consequences that may result from bearing witness to this tragedy.

It can be powerful for a group of traumatized individuals to define their own community and work together to create a safe environment, disclose experiences, and share coping strategies. While we know that education, support, and quality treatment are vital components of individual healing, it's also true that a social foundation for support and collaborative decisions about evolving concerns is invaluable. This strategy worked for both the Sandy Hook School staff and parents of surviving students. Connecting with others in a structured way to talk about fears and anxiety about the future was like a life preserver in a turbulent sea.

Sharing the successes and failures of their children's recoveries with one another and a professional helped everyone understand whether they'd witnessed a trauma reaction or normal childhood development. This also helped prevent overreactions and minimization of incidents. Generally speaking, recognizing the need to regularly attend to the healing process proved to be a strong path to resiliency.

CHAPTER TEN

EMERGENCY RESPONDERS

The catchall "first responders" typically includes police, fire departments, and the emergency medical services (EMS)/ ambulance corps. In Newtown, all of those first responders were affected, but in different ways due to varying levels of involvement. There was only one wounded teacher who needed medical assistance. She went to the hospital, so there was little need for EMS on the scene. We later learned that local hospital staff had prepped and readied for an onslaught of gunshot victims, yet tragically, their expertise was not required.

The surviving children from SHS were taken to a fire station near the school, and parents met their children there. It was frantic—a flurry of confusing activity mixed with cries of relief and anguish as the reality of the situation hit. Local and state law enforcement and emergency medical personnel were assigned to either attend to the massacre in the school or to the individuals and families at the firehouse. There was no escaping the tragedy's immediate, horrific aftermath.

The Newtown Police Department consisted of approximately forty-five officers who, along with the EMS teams, had quickly descended on the scene. The police communications team was the first to hear about the incident, having received the original 911 call. Police officers arrived less than three minutes later; describing the division of labor, one officer said, "Some of us were sent into the school to take care of the dead, while some of us stayed outside to take care of the living." The first officers to arrive entered the school and immediately saw the bodies of the principal and psychologist. In a short period of time they came upon Adam Lanza lying dead along with the bodies of several first grade children and teachers.

Additional officers were assigned to enter the school and assess the casualties, while a separate group stood guard outside and attended to parents and neighbors who rushed to the school upon hearing the news. Within minutes, Connecticut state troopers joined the scene. These officers helped secure the area, evacuated children and staff, and kept bystanders away from the crime scene. Later, and for the next several days, Newtown police detectives inventoried evidence on the school grounds. Because of the nature of the tragedy, officers who went into the school following the shooting had different debriefing efforts than officers who stayed outside. The message given to all police—those who went into the building and those who did not—was that they were not to talk to each other about their experiences. This caused division between rank-and-file officers and department leadership.

Local news coverage still included stories about the ongoing pain and anguish suffered by first responders a year and a half later, when our team formed. They suffered from flashbacks, anxiety, and negative emotional changes. Some police spoke to the media about the indelible images of these children and their teachers lying dead amid their backpacks and artwork. We heard quiet accounts of officers struggling, and that their families felt unsure how to support them. The concerns of these courageous individuals who kept the town safe and did jobs that could result in exposure to additional tragedy and death could not be ignored. Their needs, though not readily expressed to the public, needed to be embraced, but more concern was directed outside the first responder community, which meant few recovery efforts were organized for this group.

This was surprising given the magnitude of the tragedy, the size of first responder departments, and the knowledge therapists have had about first responder PTSD since the collapse of the World Trade Center in 2001. In the clinical community we know that exposure to trauma in a mass community can cause long-term distress. Reports surfaced ten years after the 9/11 attack indicating that first responders continued to struggle with mental and physical health issues related to PTSD. They reported long-term suffering, including depression, generalized anxiety disorder, and substance abuse—symptoms that still cause significant impairment in daily functioning many years after the exposure.

When we learned that the first responder community may not have received appropriate mental health services, it was safe to assume that they were highly impacted and would have multiple needs. We thought they would be open to recovery support then, and also knew that the effort would only be effective if it involved the entire department, meaning a mandatory participation order had to come from the top. After a mass tragedy, the first responder leadership may be so impacted, however, that they cannot embrace the needs of their rank-and-file staff. This appeared to be the case in Newtown.

It was also clear that the families of first responders needed help, too, because whenever you work with that community to address trauma-related issues, you must engage their families as well.

The Department of Justice grant had funds earmarked for recovery services for the local police department. These funds were embedded in expenditures that included money for other concrete items, such as security guards at each school. I assumed there was a broad awareness of these line items, and our recovery efforts would be embraced. But when I spoke with the police chief to set up an initial meeting to discuss perceived needs, he diverted me to the police wellness committee, saying that it would be a natural fit for their work and that they could provide me with guidance. I made a phone call and invited myself to the committee's next meeting, yet I learned that they had not met in some time and did not plan to meet regularly. This committee consisted of approximately half a dozen members of the rank and file; there were no managers or administrators involved.

I had hoped we would have a transparent discussion on the recovery services that had already occurred or were in place presently, and their needs going forward. I wanted to provide positive assistance, but what I encountered at the next committee meeting was different than I expected. There was a high level of resistance; I was viewed as an outsider who would never understand their experience. More shocking, though, was the repeated sentiment that recovery efforts were not needed, and that nobody in the department would participate in services or take advantage of our resources. Newtown police did not want to be thought of as heroes or victims, I was told. What they did want was a discussion about other systemic departmental issues, and to address the sense that their input was not valued in talks about grant fund allocations for police.

Unwisely, I mentioned the amount of money we had received and explained that two-thirds of the first responder fund was designated to bolster security in the community. This unleashed fierce disapproval, with more than one committee member alleging that the town did not support the department. They spoke of divides in the department, and longstanding issues made worse by the tragedy. Strong opinions simmered concerning the tactical response to the shooting, and other decisions perceived to be inadequate by staff. The frustration and disenfranchisement was palpable. For instance, they reported resentment that it took governing officials a full twenty days after the shooting to address first responders in any way. When a department has outstanding issues regarding structure, leadership, and hierarchy, and then a mass tragedy hits, existing wounds are often deepened beyond repair.

Our recovery team knew that first responders needed to be assessed and provided services. The question was how to penetrate this tight-knit community; they would not accept assistance from just anyone. I brought this dilemma to the police chief and a police union representative and gathered what I thought was enough information to understand the departmental tensions and get the committee to focus on recovery efforts to help fellow officers and make inroads regarding their other concerns. I hoped that fostering recovery might be a catalyst to larger change in the department. But when I showed up to a second committee meeting, I was the only one there. Everyone else had cancelled.

APPROPRIATE AND EFFECTIVE WORK WITH FIRST RESPONDERS

Recovery from trauma is a long process, yet the long-term needs of the affected people often fall by the wayside once public attention fades. What's more, although they are central to disaster recovery, first responder's needs are regularly neglected. They are mandated by duty to prioritize the community's needs above their own. And although typically more exposed to trauma, first responders are difficult to intervene with because they are somewhat insular.

Two years after the Sandy Hook shooting, Newtown's first responders were still suffering. They had a strong presence in the community and were instrumental in keeping the town safe and well—heroes who people turned to for direction and guidance. Their recovery was vital to Newtown's recovery as a whole. For this reason, we had to find a way to successfully approach their recovery. Many first responders were frustrated and resistant to outside help. The town's political leaders did not understand their needs. The services they had received at the time were limited and ineffective. Some efforts were supported by the police department's Employee Assistance Provider (EAP), a program to fund personal issues such as marital counseling, anger management counseling, or substance abuse treatment. Newtown police who spoke with me distrusted these services, which they said could not adequately address their needs. Some felt concerned about the services' confidentiality and spoke of past promises for change that were not followed through on.

Traditional therapeutic services did not appeal to them, since they took enormous pride in continuing their work regardless of trauma exposure. That belief system did not allow for vulnerability, which could make them ineffective at their jobs. First responders said they would rather see resources go to other members of the community than accept them for their own recovery.

In my search for an organization that might have a positive impact on our first responders, I remembered hearing that an organization called HEART 9/11 had provided assistance in the immediate aftermath of the shooting. When I asked about their presence, I received positive feedback. This is a national group that offers communities comfort and wisdom while speaking the first responder language. HEART 9/11 (Healing Emergency Aid Response Team 9/11) are former New York City first responders who came together in the aftermath of September 11th with a mission to provide immediate support to populations afflicted by natural or man-made disasters by helping rebuild infrastructure and encouraging resiliency for individuals, families, and communities. They travel around the world as volunteers to address recovery issues for highly affected first responders.

When I reached out to the organization, they were unsurprised by the feedback I'd received. I asked them to put together a proposal for Newtown. They created a comprehensive program that included four phases and would take a year to complete. The organization's president believed that not doing the work in its entirety would be more damaging than effective. They wanted a funding commitment for all four phases. Their second requirement was that the work would be confidential and kept within the police department. I would not be privy to their findings, including assessments of individual officers, or their suggestions to adjust the structure and functioning of the department as a whole.

Eventually, I secured most of the funding needed to host HEART 9/11. Leaders of the Sandy Hook Promise, The Newtown Resiliency

Center, The Newtown/Sandy Hook Community Foundation, The Parent Connection, and the United Way of Western Connecticut were all strong advocates for first responder recovery efforts. Each entity contributed money, and an angel donor wrote a $100,000 check to fill the funding gap.

MANAGING EXISTING PROGRAMMING

With the EAP provider still under contract with the police department, I worried that we might run into territorial issues. I talked with the EAP about focusing their efforts on department leadership to spark awareness of their unique needs, and the EAP agreed to formulate a Leadership Coaching Program for the police department's top brass. It would involve working with department heads to facilitate positive change, particularly in the areas of communication and cohesion. Surveys of all police staff would be conducted, and confidential meetings would take place. The hope was that new strategies would be proposed and embraced. Through some uncomfortable discussions with the police chief, it was also agreed upon that letting rank-and-file officers know that the administration was engaging in its own counseling and guidance sessions would go a long way toward promoting participation and good intent.

The EAP efforts ran simultaneous to phase one of the HEART 9/11 program.

THE ROLE OF HEART 9/11

The following is an outline of the program we created with HEART 9/11. It began with embedding their volunteers in the work and social life of Newtown's police community in order to build familiarity and trust. Slowly, through that process, the department came around. We began receiving calls from individual police officers, asking, "Can you tell me how to find a specific HEART 9/11 worker? Do you have a schedule for all of them?" We also got calls from spouses, saying, "You know, I'd like to talk to somebody."

In the end, we had close to 96 percent participation, which I was very pleased with. We even succeeded at getting the police chief and captain to work closely with HEART 9/11 and engage in dialogue and services for the greater good of the entire department.

PHASE 1: ENGAGEMENT AND ASSESSMENT

This phase was set to last eight to sixteen weeks. At first I was skeptical about what seemed like a very casual approach to starting the program. However, it was exactly what was needed to bring the first responder community around, and could not be rushed. The premise was that HEART 9/11 volunteers would integrate themselves in the first responder community slowly, to build trust and rapport. The volunteers came to Newtown for two to three days each week. They stayed at a hotel minutes away from town, and were available to people on all shifts. The volunteers were men and woman skilled at engaging officers, detectives, leadership, communications personnel, and administrators alike. They showed up at roll call and hung out in the police department lounge. They started with informal conversations and then made themselves available at a local restaurant for beer and pizza after work. They went on ride-alongs and attended community events. In short, they literally met fellow responders where they were.

Along with engaging first responders, they emphasized building rapport with the individuals' significant others. Spouses, partners, and family members often confront the results of trauma at home, but lack the first responders' camaraderie and sense of belonging to a group. Though they share experiences, many first responder families are not connected. HEART 9/11 worked to create supportive and educational meetings for family members. This would allow a support network to grow.

After about eight weeks, I started receiving calls and visits from officers and detectives asking when a certain volunteer might be back in town. My staff heard from spouses and family members asking if they could set up time to talk with a volunteer. The walls of resistance seemed to break down, and important discussions surfaced. They admitted there were recovery needs that could and should be addressed.

I stayed completely behind the scenes and let HEART 9/11 run the show. Bill Keegan, the HEART 9/11 president, met with me regularly to provide status updates and discuss logistical needs, but he kept me out of the loop beyond that to preserve confidentiality. It was truly remarkable to see first responders transform from frustrated and resistant to willing to embrace help and guidance. I did not receive commitments to participate in future activities, but was reminded by Bill that this was expected, and shouldn't dictate the project goals.

During this phase, HEART 9/11 volunteers began assessment screenings with first responders to get a more accurate picture of the police department in general, and the mental health of the officers specifically. The assessment screens informed decisions about where to focus resources. They identified concerns, like the need for better substance abuse counseling and anger management training. Overall, the tool was developed to measure challenges and strategize for future improvements in the following areas:

- Department Effectiveness
- Individual Functioning
- Family Unit Functioning
- Community Engagement

The assessment tool was explained and distributed to officers at roll call. There was follow-up during breaks, and it was collected over a period of weeks. The survey was voluntary and confidential. It included self-reporting measures, open-ended questions, and a place to record conversations between facilitators, first responders, and significant others in either individual or group settings.

HEART 9/11 collected the data at three different intervals: the initial assessment, an intervention phase, and a three-month follow-up post-intervention phase. The data was reviewed only by HEART 9/11 and police department heads. I did not see it because of our confidentiality agreement. Yet I had complete faith in the group's healing process. Trust was important to their effort, because if police officers had believed that outsiders would learn about their personal struggles and challenges, they would never have participated.

PHASE 2: INTERVENTION

This component focused on individual and group recovery. It involved weekend retreats for first responders and their significant others, which offered the opportunity for family fun while also providing a venue for sharing their trauma experience through storytelling and bonding activities. The retreats included activities such as a cooking contest, fireside relaxation, mindfulness mini-workshops, yoga, and tai chi. There was time for educational information about trauma and recovery, as well as individual and couples support. HEART 9/11 clearly recognized that families have a vital role to play in the recovery process as a source of strength and support. They also knew family members could be highly impacted themselves and should not be overlooked. Workshops in relationship rebuilding and parenting skills were conducted as well.

For this phase, the HEART 9/11 facilitators brought along members with clinical backgrounds. The participants helped choose activities and the location, dates, and timeframe (one, two, or three days). This promoted buy-in and a sense of empowerment.

We held several retreats to accommodate the majority of the police department. My team provided assistance in organizing, purchasing necessary items, and recruiting instructors for yoga and other activities. These retreats were unique because everyone present had been affected by a mass tragedy and shared trauma. That environment allowed for big-picture questions to be directed to people who understood, having lived the first responder role themselves.

I believe these retreats helped build a healthier environment within the police force and decreased fracturing within the department. Officers and their families were provided a safe space to share their feelings about the initial event and their ongoing challenges living with the impact of trauma. HEART 9/11 gave me only the most general statistics, but I could tell that relationships within the department were improving. In the end, the police chief sent me a beautiful letter thanking me for facilitating this unique and important program.

PHASE 3: REBUILD

This involved construction projects that first responders worked on together to demonstrate their ongoing ability to help others. The premise of this phase was that it's essential to resiliency to change feelings of helplessness after a traumatic event. The rebuild projects empowered first responders by reinforcing that they had control in their lives. The completed buildings also stood as a tangible reminder that they could make changes in their lives and use the tragedy as a platform to grow. Their experiences were used to give back to others, and in doing so, heal themselves.

Much of this phase took place after the NRRT had completed its grant work and disbanded. The group chose to do a construction project that would benefit veterans in a neighboring state. They also participated in renovations to a farm, making it suitable for family retreats and ongoing sustainable farming. The intended outcome of this phase was to enhance the healing process by moving outside of the immediate community to assist others. Doing this strengthens connections, and the networking scope widens. First responders will have learned to recognize the emotional and physical impact trauma exposure had on them, and share their experiences and healing journey success through contributing to the wellness of others. The concept is to pay it forward and mentor others in the aftermath of a traumatic event.

PHASE 4: CONTINUING CONNECTIONS

This phase was about moving forward and perpetuating the recovery network. In recovery, we never think of our efforts and activities as being "one and done." We wanted the recovery work to sustain itself well after our team disbanded, and this phase illustrated that concept for the first responder community. Its leaders were provided mental health awareness training and leadership workshops. The goal was to teach first responders to recognize signs of psychological distress in their department and community, and how to support them and recommend appropriate services when necessary.

After the NRRT disbanded, I kept up with Bill Keegan regarding the progress of the program. He informed me of its continued success. Some officers became deeply involved in the recovery process and assumed leadership roles involving continued education. The organization's volunteers are still in touch with the Newtown police department, and in fact several of its officers joined the HEART 9/11 team.

I had started this journey with a first responder community filled with resistance, frustration, and profound challenges regarding a need for change, so this was a poignant wrap to a lengthy project. Adjustments were made to the police department management, and it felt like our work would have a lasting impact, with structural changes coinciding with individuals feeling empowered to include recovery and resiliency in their culture in a sustainable way. Attitudes seemed to shift from excluding dialogue about emotional needs to admission that attention must be paid to this.

IN SUMMARY

It's important to remember you can't simply walk in and introduce services to first responders. These individuals take pride in doing their job despite trauma exposure. Their ethos does not allow for vulnerability, which is assumed to make them less effective in their work. Impacted individuals can become severely isolated, then, if the broader first responder community does not embrace seeking help and guidance. In Newtown this is what happened. Recovery efforts need to occur from the top down, but often after a mass tragedy, department leaders are so impacted themselves they cannot embrace the needs of their rank-and-file staff.

This proud, dedicated group of police officers would rather have given its recovery funding to other community groups. Sensitivity to their culture was key to successful engagement, and we learned that it was important to manage their recovery program from behind the scenes since we are not their peers and would not have been accepted into their circle. In the end, 96 percent of the police department participated in the recovery programming.

HEART 9/11 taught us the key to working with the first responder community was to craft a thoughtful long-term recovery plan that involved over three months of pure engagement work. We also learned that families of first responders should not be forgotten. When addressing trauma-related issues, you must engage and work with the families as well.

CHAPTER ELEVEN

SUPPORTING CLINICIANS, CLERGY, AND PEDIATRICIANS

The NRRT was tasked with providing services for the entire town, and as a result, we had the unique ability to ask groups of helping professions what their needs and concerns were for both themselves and for the communities they served. Every time I collaborated with a local clinician, clergy member, or pediatrician, I asked, "What else can we do? What do you need?" Most often, the suggestions centered on the community, not on themselves.

The grant and our subsequent community needs assessment mentioned that helping professionals needed help too. However, there were no guidelines on how to engage or prepare programming for their unique challenges. Like the first responder community, many of these professionals were trained to focus on other's needs—to help people achieve physical, emotional, and spiritual wellness—so they were inclined to minimize their own struggles, absorbed as they were in the responsibility to support a community in crisis.

We met these practitioners while the care coordinators built our resource bank. We befriended them individually, hearing about their experiences, strengths, and challenges, and as we familiarized ourselves with available therapeutic practices and directed individuals to treatments, we got the impression that many practitioners were not evaluating their own needs. Again, this is commonplace in the clinical world. While most clinicians practice self-care, it is easy to get caught up with a sense of duty to your client, or in this case an obligation to your community, that results in little time or energy to think about what you need and find support among colleagues.

Since this was new territory, I had little knowledge of what might be valuable to them. I could only ask and offer to create avenues to ease their challenges. We did this successfully, I think, despite our limited time and resources. We developed programs targeting each of these professional groups, and through them we learned that these individuals need a safe environment to ask questions in, and hear others in the same role provide answers.

The following are examples of the programs we developed.

ADDRESSING THE NEEDS OF MENTAL HEALTH CLINICIANS

When we asked clinicians about their challenges, we began to understand what the community and their colleagues faced. Some clinicians drove in from out of state to set up a weekly practice because their services were not otherwise locally available, and they believed they could make a difference. Some had part-time practices before the shooting, yet now operated on a full-time basis. Some clinicians worked for agencies, others in group practices, and some were independent. The majority lived locally, had children in Newtown schools, attended local sporting events and religious services, and lived in neighborhoods where reminders of the community's change and loss were prevalent.

No matter where the clinicians came from, they all believed it their responsibility to help others. And while most practitioners had expertise in trauma-informed care and grief work, the dynamics of many cases associated with the shooting brought on symptomology of complicated grief and acute trauma, which are always challenging. Many stretched themselves professionally and personally. However, when we came on the scene, no collaboration or mutual support had occurred among these practitioners.

As a first step, I organized a providers meeting. This would be an opportunity for everyone to meet and familiarize themselves with one another's treatment work. It also allowed our team to register practitioners who had not yet spoken with us and get their information in our resource database. Most importantly, participants had a chance to discuss challenges, ask questions about policies like reimbursement protocols, and inform us of how we could help foster a healthy clinical community.

The meeting was well attended. Everyone seemed eager to hear about our team and learn about a new system to bring them referrals and assist clients in navigating their mental health needs. We opened up for questions and discussed the current state of practice, sharing perspectives on what might help moving forward. Many clinicians and practitioners were themselves struggling with emotional overload.

There was plenty of trauma and grief work to go around. For some, the personal calling to help as many people as they could left them feeling guilty when someone had to be turned away. Others lamented that it was impossible to get away from the heaviness of the work, particularly if you lived in Newtown and went home to families who were also impacted by the tragedy. One practitioner who drove in from out of state expressed acute PTSD and traumatic response, saying, "I know this is impacting me, because as soon as I pass the Sandy Hook exit sign on the highway I feel a tremendous heaviness, as if a cloud is looming all the time."

Through this initial meeting we created a wish list that could help make this group's work a little easier. They seemed relieved that we would be available to help as a liaison in the billing and reimbursement arena, and that any client we sent to them would be followed by a care coordinator, who would assist in navigating treatment needs. There was enthusiasm as we discussed the potential to provide educational workshops and ongoing support.

I introduced the idea of small supervision and/or support groups. We heard positive feedback, though also concerns about scheduling, and anxiety over committing to yet more appointments in their already packed schedules. Most of the practitioners already struggled to manage their days. There wasn't enough time to care for their clients and families, let alone themselves. We had to be cognizant of this while fostering continued growth and connectedness. We did not want to create more stress, or push anyone away with overt pressure to participate.

This initial meeting expanded our registry to over 150 treatment providers. We then created educational workshops we believed would be relevant and valuable. Two were exclusive to clinicians, but we invited everyone on the registry to join all of our community programs.

The first workshop was titled "Existential Trauma." The presenter was David Grand, PhD, an author, lecturer, and clinician who specialized in the brainspotting technique, which proved to be a breakthrough treatment for many individuals in the community experiencing trauma reactions. David had been coming to Newtown since the shooting and was already donating his time to treat patients. At the workshop, he presented his theories on brain-based work and demonstrated strategies that combine brainspotting techniques with cognitive work. He also discussed the way vicarious trauma likely played out for every clinician involved in the recovery effort, and allowed for thoughtful discussion, case sharing, and questions.

Almost a hundred practitioners attended David's program, and we heard them say it was very educational, but of particular value were the discussions with colleagues about shared clinical experiences. Participants learned it's important to think about the mind-body connection and neurobiological impact when treating trauma.

Several months later we offered a second practitioner's workshop, titled "Trauma Stewardship." The concept was that you must identify the effects of living with constant exposure to trauma, and subsequently take better care of yourself. When you master this self-care practice, you become a model, or "steward," for others. During our last six months we focused on this idea, hoping to bring it home for the entire community that everyone should take better care of themselves. It was time to think about what resiliency really means and embrace it. This was particularly true for helping professionals.

For the programming, we invited the author of a book on trauma stewardship to conduct a few days of presentations with several groups. Laura van Dernoot Lipsky's work fit our message of recognizing your own needs in order to heal and move in a resilient direction. During her time in Newtown, Laura gave separate presentations to clinicians, town leaders, Sandy Hook School staff, and the community at large.

We also wanted to educate the community about the services of the professionals we were referring people to. We did this by involving the mental health clinicians and healing professionals in two other events. The first was "Passport to Wellness," an event for municipal employees. Practitioners spent the afternoon in the town hall showcasing and actually practicing their service on participants. It was truly an experiential day. The second event was a community-wide mental health awareness fair. Clinicians set up tables with information and handouts for all attendees, so they could better understand the different treatment modalities available. There was a panel discussion and lots of take-away items, including a booklet our team published highlighting effective mental health and trauma-based treatments, and questions to ask when choosing a therapist.

Finally, we launched a peer support and supervision group for clinical practitioners. Our center was open to them for biweekly meetings where they discussed concerns and shared information about interesting topics and differing perspectives on difficult cases. It also provided an opportunity to disclose clinical and personal challenges or exchange strategies. The group struggled at first to find its footing and adopt a format everyone was comfortable with. But today, several years after the initial group meeting, some of the clinicians continue to meet on a monthly basis. I am still a member, and have found it invaluable. It is a safe place to discuss cases as well as the current political landscape and how it affects our work.

SUPPORTING THE CLERGY

The pastor of Newtown Congregational Church served on my board of directors, and I asked him if we could support clergy and other faith-based leaders in town. He relayed my offer to a longstanding interfaith clergy group. They felt that they were adequately supporting each other already. However, they thought it would be helpful to come together to discuss difficulties within their communities.

I reached out to Lisa Cataldo, PhD, a professor at Fordham University I met through a group producing a documentary about the Sandy Hook School shooting. She teaches religion and psychology, and is the author of two books that address relational perspectives on trauma, dissociation, and faith. She agreed to visit Newtown to present her theories and mediate a discussion with local clergy. The final result was a workshop for interfaith leaders that incorporated both educational and experiential components, as well as a discussion and sharing of experiences. The focus included:

- How is faith functioning in the aftermath of the tragedy?
- Traumatic events can hurt an individual's relationship to God. How do you assist them in their religious and spiritual experience from the perspective of a traumatized self?
- How do you support those who are dissociated and/or defensive about their religion?

- How do you recognize natural fragmentation and
  invite all the fragmented parts to be repaired through
  a faith-based approach?
- What can we teach and what would be helpful as we
  continue to move forward?
- What is the faithful person's healing trajectory? What is
  normal? How can ritual or culture help?

This presentation was attended by approximately ten clergy members, which represented most of the town's religious leadership. I considered inviting individuals from neighboring communities, including congregational leaders who made significant donations or had a helpful impact during the first months after the tragedy. But the Newtown interfaith group wanted to keep this project within their own intimate group.

We brought in lunch and allowed Lisa to create a safe space for attendees to talk about their experiences. Many felt conflicted about presiding over congregations in which the strengthening of faith and questioning of faith regularly interwove. Some expressed discomfort at being recognized like a celebrity when attending professional events outside their community.

The discussions seemed valuable. Following a community tragedy, local clergy open their doors to those needing a place to pray and reflect. They also grapple with issues that transcend grief and mourning, questions that pose spiritual challenges. How do you turn sorrow and sympathy into solidarity and action? How do you provide clarity in the chaos of devastation? Can this tragedy be put in perspective? How do you inspire your community to move beyond its fears to a place of compassion, connection, and forgiveness? What role do you play in moving people toward personal and collective healing and growth? Are we addressing issues of safety in our houses of worship?

They all knew our team was there to support them, and were reminded of how to access our assistance. While each presiding clergy member must handle these questions for their members, it is also important to find opportunities to come together, share experiences, and help members connect and embrace those of different faiths. A wonderful example of this is an interfaith vigil that takes place each year on the anniversary of the tragedy. Flags fly at half-staff, candles are lit, and clergy and parishioners of several faiths come together to pray, connect, and express strength through faith.

REACHING AREA PEDIATRICIANS

A few months before the end of our assignment, we were granted a three-month extension. The grant budget and the town's willingness to absorb expenses allowed us to stay on to assist with the transition phase. I used this time to continue care coordination services, and compiled a report on community healing next steps, as town leaders discussed creating a wellness office. The extension also allowed me to revisit programs and pursue ideas that we didn't think there was time for. One such idea came from talks with a pediatric practice in town.

Local pediatricians had been grateful to know that our services covered the entire town, since they saw lots of patients who could be referred to us for mental health concerns. As professional helpers, they worried more about their patients than themselves, even though their practices were busier than normal. I had requested a meeting to discuss the biological aspects of trauma exposure with a pediatrician who was astute at referring patients and parents of patients to us for assessment of their emotional well-being. During our conversation, we realized we didn't know if Newtown doctors were well versed in this research.

It was unclear what issues might arise five, ten, or twenty years after the tragedy, but studies indicated that there would be some impact, and that options were available to predict, and possibly prevent, that negative trajectory of medical and mental health conditions from developing. We wanted to present the latest screening tools to them and promote utilization. This pediatrician introduced us to the now famous Adverse Childhood Experiences (ACE) Study and its resulting questionnaire. A groundbreaking research project conducted by Kaiser Permanente and the Centers for Disease Control and Prevention (CDC) in 1998, this was the first large-scale research into the relationship between ten categories of adversity in childhood, including trauma exposure, and health outcomes in adulthood. It revealed that:

> Childhood experiences, both positive and negative, have a tremendous impact on future violence victimization and perpetration, and lifelong health and opportunity. As such, early experiences are an important public health issue. Adverse Childhood Experiences have been linked to risky health behaviors, chronic health conditions, low life potential, and early death. As the number of ACEs increases, so does the risk for these outcomes.

I decided to bring awareness of this topic to the local pediatric community. It made sense to promote this theory, if only to spark thoughts on incorporating resources to address emotional concerns into traditional medical visits.

The Child Health and Development Institute of Connecticut (CHDI) had a program that addressed this issue. Their Educating Practices In the Community (EPIC) program offered seventeen training modules to improve the content and delivery of child health services by assisting providers in implementing practice changes. This was a natural answer to questions that arose concerning long-term emotional and physical impacts from the traumatic event, such as: Are there actions doctors can take to prevent these negative outcomes? What questions should pediatricians be asking? When is it appropriate to intervene? What recommendations should be made?

The two modules that matched our agenda were "Behavioral Health Screening: Integration into Pediatric Primary Care," and "Trauma Screening: Identification and Referral in Pediatric Practice." The executive director of CHDI was excited to collaborate and provide technical training to Newtown's pediatric community. This felt like an important transition. While so much of our work addressed present, immediate needs, this was an opportunity to impact long-term needs in a preventative manner.

Finally, through a few more discussions, it was suggested that I engage the local hospital's pediatric medicine department. This was the hospital that received, processed, and treated victims and survivors of the shooting. We scheduled a presentation during the hospital's grand rounds. In partnership with the CHDI, we offered a two-part workshop titled "Trauma Screening and Behavioral Health Interventions for Pediatrics."

I marketed the series to local physicians through a mailer and followed up with phone calls and in-person meetings. The hospital also marketed the series to staff, and the event was well attended. The training and subsequent discussion informed them how to incorporate trauma screenings into a pediatric exam, as well as the next steps to take if an exam screened positive.

If we'd had more time in the community, we would have continued to focus on this agenda. Our grant did not address the integration of research and prevention, though it became apparent that while we could not eliminate exposure to traumatic events, we could get better at predicting their physical and emotional impacts, and put appropriate supports and services in place to minimize these negative outcomes. This is particularly important for the youngest among us.

IN SUMMARY

The individuals who people turn to for help in times of crisis also need recovery support. The stronger these clinical, medical, and spiritual leaders are, the stronger the community is. Often, though, these groups forget to evaluate the impact that living, breathing, and working in a traumatized community has on them.

Talking about challenges and struggles is not a sign of weakness. We found time and again that people felt empowered sharing and validating each other's experiences. Without this, their difficult work could be emotionally draining.

Vicarious trauma is impossible to escape when your daily practice is laden with stories of grief and need. Coming together to discuss the challenges that come from absorbing these stories day after day is invaluable. It felt as if we helped create a greater sense of connection within these microcosms of the community at large. As a recovery leader, you are in a unique position to bring these groups together for education and support. Many patients, clients, or congregants will also be better served for it.

CHAPTER TWELVE

THE IMPORTANCE
OF SELF-CARE

One of the most challenging aspects of working with a community forever changed by a tragic event is that the trauma effects are widespread and individualized at the same time. This was compounded by constant news stories about the investigation, political and community decisions, heroism, and loss. The public wanted to glean every new bit of information it could, and hear accounts of those who survived this tragedy, but knowing more details of the event didn't lessen its impact. On the contrary, it spurred more questions and concerns. Scientists Roxane Cohen Silver, PhD, and E. Alison Holman, PhD, studied the emotional effects of news coverage of tragedies like the 9/11 terror attacks and the Boston Marathon bombing, and they suspect that "extended, repetitive media exposure keeps the event alive in one's conscious awareness, and in so doing may turn what was an acute stress into a chronic stressor, with the potential for long-term physiological consequences."

While the coverage may have been informative and stirred up support for the community, it also left many feeling even more alone in their grief. We searched for a program and a presenter who could deliver a concrete message on the importance of adopting a regular practice of self-care through an honest firsthand account. I wasn't interested in an expert merely educating the audience; I wanted a person who could meet people where they were in their individual recovery journey and open up a greater awareness and discussion about how to move forward individually and embrace the work necessary to take care of the community's needs. At the suggestion of my trauma specialist, we brought the concept of trauma stewardship to Newtown. Trauma stewardship was developed by Laura van Dernoot Lipsky, who realized while working with survivors of child abuse, domestic violence, sexual assault, and other acute traumas, that her ability to live a healthy life was impaired by secondary trauma. To sustain her work, she had to learn to identify her needs, adopt a plan for self-care, and then assist neighbors, clients, and colleagues with their own trauma.

Her concepts seemed relevant to stories we heard from every facet of the community. In Newtown, as in most communities impacted by tragic events, efforts to support recovery took not just a village, but a nation. The helpers came in all shapes and sizes. They were community leaders thrust into the limelight who worked tirelessly to address the town's overwhelming needs. They were families and neighbors, teachers and first responders, experts and organizations, doctors, clinicians, coaches, and business owners. They were children and grandparents. They were clergy, funeral directors, and anonymous donors. They were the millions of people around the world who wrote letters, sent money, and held vigils far away from Newtown. They were the local and national news reporters who continued to remind the world that this tragedy should not be forgotten, that the suffering was far reaching, that it would be long-term, and that such a dark event brought forward bravery, hope, and healing as well. All of the individuals I've mentioned ended up being impacted in some way as they responded to those more obviously in need. But not all of them took care of themselves.

To bring awareness to the avoidance of self-care by professionals and community members in the healing realm, it's important to educate the public about vicarious trauma and the self-care options available to people impacted by trauma, whether they are two or ten steps removed from the tragic circumstances.

UNDERSTANDING VICARIOUS TRAUMA

While no community members are immune to the impact of a massive tragedy, those whose work exposes them to residual or secondary trauma are particularly susceptible to negative impacts. Secondary trauma is indirect exposure to trauma through hearing firsthand accounts of the event. The survivor's vivid description of their experience can affect the listener cognitively and emotionally, sometimes resulting in symptoms that parallel those of someone diagnosed with PTSD. Even as we focus on helping others heal and move forward, we often lose sight of how this work transforms us. There are several terms for this: shared trauma, vicarious trauma, or compassion fatigue.

Without question, "holding space" with trauma victims and individuals working through grief creates an environment in which the clinician may absorb pain and distress. It is impossible to work in a community impacted by a traumatic event without experiencing significant psychological changes. At the very least, secondary exposure creates exhaustion and burnout, which is why self-care is important. Without it, professionals can experience lasting negative effects to their health and wellness.

The following professional and personal changes can indicate that you are not practicing adequate self-care and are operating in an unhealthy manner.

- You no longer feel energized at home or work.
- Your job has become all-consuming, with no balance between work, family, and play.
- You lose objectivity. Either your clients' issues are a larger-than-life priority, or you feel numb to their dilemmas.
- You no longer devote time to your support network, such as family and friends.
- Your leisure activities are no longer leisurely. You either put no effort into them, or you act ultra-competitive, taking these activities to the extreme.
- After a stressful day, you indulge in unhealthy substances.
- You lose your sense of humor and feel sad or angry all the time.
- You cut corners at work and don't care if it catches up to you.
- Work feels unrewarding.
- You experience frequent headaches, stomachaches, or other physical concerns.

- You isolate yourself to avoid exposing others to your irritability or depression.
- You isolate yourself because you are too exhausted to interact with people outside of your work.
- You have a hard time concentrating, make mistakes, and forget things.
- You find yourself staring into space or feel disinterested in your work.
- The people closest to you allude to changes they have noticed in your behaviors.
- Nothing feels enjoyable.

TRAUMA STEWARDSHIP

Laura van Dernoot Lipsky's work on trauma stewardship informed my thinking about the importance of self-care. She defines the concept as "a daily practice through which individuals, organizations, and societies tend to the hardship, pain, or trauma experienced by humans, other living beings, or our planet itself." Those who support trauma stewardship believe that joy and pain are both realities of life, yet suffering can be transformed into meaningful growth and healing when there is an awareness of its effect and you work to regain balance and be present in your life rather than walk through it in a state of numbness. Trauma stewardship also addresses the cumulative effect of an individual's trauma exposure on their community and asks, "How do you consistently help yourself and pay it forward to help others by modeling self-care?"

It is especially important for professionals who provide direct care in a traumatized community to adopt this practice in their personal and professional lives. Trauma stewardship should be a point of focus, not an afterthought as is so often the case.

We brought Laura to Newtown to deliver this message personally and demonstrate to several groups the power of self-care. The final months of our work seemed like the right time for the community to hear her message. Trauma stewardship is first and foremost about purposeful care and spiritual balance, and secondly about modeling this mindful approach while absorbing the suffering of others. It is our responsibility to understand our vulnerabilities. This concept seemed to be the perfect antidote to job-related concerns we heard from clinicians and teachers through our workshops.

STRATEGIES FOR DEALING WITH VICARIOUS TRAUMA

Life is busy, but declining to pause is sometimes a cover-up to avoid painful or dysregulating personal reflections. It can feel as if the only way to function when we absorb so much distress is to push forward—keeping it together in order to hold others' hands. Yet there are strategies to alleviate the negative psychological and physical impacts on wellness when immersed in recovery work. Often the most important and overlooked aspect is mindfulness. How does this demanding, highly stressful work impact you? Through awareness and focus, compassion fatigue can be minimized, while compassion satisfaction—a feeling of pleasure, positive momentum, and balance—is elevated.

Self-care should start with an assessment of areas of your life that may be stretched. If physical and emotional changes occur, take note of sacrifices you have made. For instance, it's common for individuals working with trauma to experience insomnia. A healthy diet may be pushed aside because of a lack of time to prepare nourishing meals. Next, assess whether you get regular exercise, spend quality time with friends and family, and participate in mindfulness activities such as meditation or yoga. If religion and/or spiritual connections have been important in the past, are you still engaged in those activities? Setting healthy limits at work and home is also important. Saying "no" when you realize you are already overloaded is something most of us avoid, yet can have major consequences for the way we feel about our work and ourselves.

Being strong for others involves acknowledging your own vulnerabilities and setting as much time aside to take care of yourself as you do for others. This must be a priority. Feeling nervous, scared, uncomfortable, and helpless is part of the work; don't ignore those emotions, believing you merely have to work through them. Instead, address your fears. Acknowledge discomfort, and most importantly have compassion for yourself. Practice the self-care that you preach.

HOW TO PRACTICE SELF-CARE

Proper self-care involves a range of activities that promote a balance between personal and professional roles. Making your own well-being a priority allows you to make healthy choices for the people you serve, and if you are unable to replenish your resources, to refresh your own mind and body, you cannot effectively model a healthy balance. From now on:

- Identify activities that make you feel positive energy or resilience.
- Block out time on your calendar to engage in these activities.

- Whenever there is an opportunity to engage in a mindfulness activity, do it. Take a walk at lunchtime. Go out to eat with a colleague. Take a hot bath after a long day. Get on the floor and play with your pets, or your children. Journal, sing, be creative, plant some flowers, or meditate.

- Take care of yourself physically. Don't skip meals. Eat healthy. Sleep well. Go to the doctor if you are feeling unwell.

- Know when to say no. Set boundaries. Don't feel the need to constantly stretch yourself. Let others take the lead, at least until you feel more in control.

- Take a self-inventory every day. Ask yourself, "Do I feel depleted? Do I need to get away from work for a bit? Am I feeling irritable, resentful, sad, or empty?"

- Surround yourself with people who are positive and enjoy life.

- Seek professional help when the light at the end of tunnel fades and you cannot figure out a way to renew it.

- Find balance. Don't let work be your only intentional activity every day, every week.

- Identify what is *good enough*. You will never erase the impact of a tragic experience for others. Find what *is* enough, instead of thinking "it's never enough."

- Find a sense of peace. This is different for everyone. Is it your deck chair with a book, a religious service, a yoga studio, or a favorite hike?

- Release the guilt. There is no place for it and it's not constructive. Helping those who have less or are more impacted than you is a phenomenon that comes with the job. Feeling guilty for their loss and devastation does not alter the situation. It only eats away at you.

- Pay it forward. Be a self-care steward. Don't just talk the talk, walk the walk, so you can promote this practice to friends and colleagues.

POST-TRAUMATIC GROWTH

We adopted the term *post-traumatic growth* as the positive goal everyone should strive for in the wake of a traumatic experience. Coined by Richard Tedeschi, PhD, and Lawrence Calhoun, PhD, post-traumatic growth is the notion that humans who experience a major crisis, like the sudden loss of a loved one, can emerge from it with some positive change. I think of post-traumatic growth (PTG) as being synonymous with resilience. It does not divert from the challenges associated with a traumatic experience; rather, PTG is the belief that you can also achieve personal growth, encounter new opportunities, develop closer relationships, gain a stronger appreciation for life, and deepen your spiritual core in the wake of tragedy.

How we manage the crisis's impact and change in ourselves will affect our ability to extract meaning and weather the transformations in a healthy way.

IN SUMMARY

Recovery professionals need a healthy work life balance to function, build resilience, and support colleagues. Self-care is often sacrificed in order to make room for helping clients, but pushing our emotional and physical wellness aside is a recipe for burnout and ineffective response. With disaster recovery needs increasing every year, we need to be acutely aware that taking care of ourselves is as important as caring for others. We can create a culture of balance and wellness by being honest about the impact this work has on us, and serve as role models for healthy boundaries and mindful living in our communities.

Resilience and post-traumatic growth are concepts everyone can strive for in the wake of trauma exposure. When the practice starts with helping professionals, it naturally trickles down to benefit everyone they connect with in the community.

CHAPTER THIRTEEN

ADDRESSING ONGOING NEEDS

Every program or service should be rolled out in a way that is sustainable. You always want your programs to be easily recreated by others once you step away. Trauma has long-term effects, and symptoms may resurface for many years, sometimes lasting a lifetime. As a clinician or recovery leader, your tangible work time is limited, but knowing that it can go on without your oversight is rewarding. This requires you to develop strong relationships with community leaders who will be in place after you leave. You also must prepare for this stage by successfully raising money and presenting data-driven reports on long-term needs.

To create the long-term fluidity that this kind of work warrants, it's necessary to collect feedback, evaluations, and suggestions for change. Even when there are a multitude of variables, thinking about potential outcomes and planning for the future is an important part of building a recovery platform. We analyzed data often to consider current and future needs for the community. Reporting the status of ongoing needs based on these projections was invaluable. The reports included information gathered from sources such as community assessments, tracking, and data collection for our clients.

Being able to produce numbers that convey trends can help secure funding too. Raising money may be the biggest challenge for continued recovery programs. In our case, it became necessary to advocate that vital services be factored into the town budget, and that foundations plan to fund certain expenses. Without careful planning, quality services may be undermined, solely due to a lack of funds. But even with funding, we had to identify specific ambassadors within the community who could help keep programs operating.

Individual recovery from a massive tragedy is a process that will ebb and flow for many years, and healing a community is no different, except that the resources are multiplied, funds can become scarce, and attention to ongoing assistance diminishes over time. Even for a recovery specialist, it is often instinctual to focus on critical and immediate needs. The grant only allowed my team to be in place for eighteen months—in itself a false message that the community would reach full resiliency in that time. All current research on clinical recovery tells us that this is not the case. In fact, a healing trajectory that begins with acute assessment and ends in resiliency can take ten to fifteen years to complete.

What I anticipated going into Sandy Hook was that I would need to plan for long-term needs from day one. Thinking about trends and changes in the recovery landscape, and creating a means to report this information, would be as valuable as addressing immediate needs. I ingrained this assumption in my team, and we adopted language to indicate awareness that this was a long-term endeavor. We spoke about recovery as an ongoing process that cannot be rushed or defined by a certain timeframe. And when introducing new programming, we often articulated hope that the work would continue after our team exited the community.

WHERE DO YOU START?

Right from the beginning, it's important to capture data regarding immediate needs and potential responses to services you will offer. The information will help to forecast the recovery trajectory so your community can plan for the future. The following questions will help you develop such a system:

- What data will you collect?
- How will you obtain that data?
- How will you evaluate the data?
- To what will you compare the data?
- How will you make the data qualitative?

Keep in mind there may not be funds allocated to gather data, staff may not be directly mandated to take this on, and most recovery personnel are not experts in data collection. Also, collecting data is not a one-time endeavor. It is an ongoing effort that should be incorporated into daily practice.

Before collecting data, you should have a clear idea of what your targets are, such as whom you are serving, how services are being received, and what outcomes result from your work. You can set goals for how you will respond to your outcomes. We did not do this, however, since I did not have a strong enough sense of the direction our work would take. If I had started with a clearer understanding of the trajectory of trauma, I would have thought more about what a successful outcome might be. Is it mere participation in recovery treatment? Is it the change or impact of the services? Is success measured by an individual's daily functioning? Is it suggested by repeat visits to the center, or rather a decline in visits? For all these theories, some baseline data would be required. We did not collect baseline data in these areas.

Our team collected data on every individual who called or came in for assistance. But I suggest you collect a limited range of data. You do not want your staff stressed out or preoccupied with data collection. Recovery work should in no way be dictated or slowed by these efforts. Data collection should be simple—a sophisticated system is not necessary. The format should be easy and allow for consistency. When formalizing your data collection system, ask yourself:

- What will the source be for each element of data? Interview questions, a formal questionnaire, symptom reports, or initial and follow-up surveys?
- Who will enter the data?
- Where will the data be stored?

On my team, all staff collected information on paper forms, and the project manager transferred the targeted elements to a software program that we developed to store the data and create reports. I wanted to understand who was coming in, what their needs were, how much funding it would take to provide necessary services, and how their requests and needs related to the tragedy. We also categorized individuals into a "person type." The following topics helped capture all this material:

- The initial reason for seeking services from the NRRT
- Services requests from those attending Sandy Hook Elementary School and outside it
- Number of cases for each person type
- Total funds paid out from the collaborative recovery fund and wellness fund monthly
- Total funds paid out from the collaborative recovery fund and wellness fund cumulatively
- New clients seeking assistance per month
- Average funds for recovery and health and wellness paid per family by person type
- Individuals requesting services by age
- Individuals requesting services by gender
- Requests for non-12/14-related services

We looked at this information regularly and created monthly and quarterly reports to present at our board meetings. The documents included graphs and charts that we distributed to board members. This allowed me to discuss our work with data that supported my analysis of what people were experiencing and how long the recovery services might need to last.

The "person type" classification was broken down and defined by the following seventeen categories:

1. Administrator or public official

2. Concerned member of the Newtown/Sandy Hook community

3. Employee or employer of a business in Sandy Hook or Newtown

4. Faith community (clergy)

5. Family member of a child or adult lost on 12/14

6. Firefighter (Newtown or other responding community)

7. Mental health or other community service provider

8. Newtown volunteer ambulance corps

9. Other responding professional on 12/14 (medical, crisis responder)

10. Parent of a child enrolled at Sandy Hook Elementary School (present or not) on 12/14

11. Parent of a child enrolled in another Newtown school (public or private)

12. Parent of a child not currently enrolled in a Newtown school (i.e. too young, already graduated, enrolled in a school out of district/in another community, etc.)

13. Police (Newtown, state, or other responding community)

14. Spouse, parent, or child of an adult witness/survivor (teacher, emergency responder)

15. Teacher or staff member employed at Sandy Hook Elementary School (present or not) on 12/14

16. Teacher or staff member in another Newtown school (public or private) on 12/14

17. Young adult (age 18-25)

Because my team provided a combination of services and resources, these reports also allowed for discussions about who was coming in, what was being funded, and how much was being spent on mental health and wellness services. Regarding groups, we considered which groups were high utilizers of services, which groups needed an alternative means of outreach since their utilization was low, and which groups needed supportive programming because service requests were high. We also captured and evaluated the type and frequency of requested services. These included:

- Mental health counseling
- Art therapy
- Music therapy
- Equine therapy
- Chiropractic care
- Gym membership
- Camp fees
- Hypnotherapy
- Kinesiology
- Bio/neurofeedback
- Somatic experiencing
- Massage therapy
- Medication management
- Medical doctor referral
- Dental referral
- Reiki
- Tapping therapy

- Social and emotional support
- Enrichment resources

We expanded our service list to include new treatments as we learned of their value. We also looked at particular service usages by person type to expand our resources and plan for the future. Eventually, we broke down these numbers into two reports—requests for services from those inside and those outside the Sandy Hook School community.

We also created several reports about funds—where the money was spent and who benefited from it. In these monthly reports, we assigned each individual a number to preserve confidentiality, and showed the amount of money spent on their personal mental health and wellness services. This report also showed the category each individual fell into, and totals regarding payout or reimbursement amounts. This allowed us to think about issues like insurance coverage, the cost of services regularly utilized by certain individuals, and expectations for funding needs for particular individuals or groups. We created an overall report, too, on monthly expenditures broken down by mental health services and what we called health and wellness services (gym memberships, camp fees, and the like).

Finally, we created reports on age and gender demographics for those seeking assistance from our team. For some communities I imagine that reporting demographics such as ethnicity, socioeconomic standing, and disability status might be important. We thought about looking at these categories, but felt that representation in the Newtown community was so small it would not provide actionable information.

SURVEY OR NEEDS ASSESSMENT DATA COLLECTION

When we created needs assessment surveys, we sought information that would provide insight into needs gaps. This allowed us to enhance offerings or change course if there was strong indication we were not adequately providing for a particular need or group. This also gave me factual data to back up verbal presentations showing that needs in the community still existed or continued to be unmet. The data showed positive trends in the community's perception of how the town was doing, on top of the respondents' own sense of hope and resiliency for the future. This survey included the following topics:

- Feelings about whether the community is moving forward
- Connections to the community
- Where individuals are finding their connections to the community
- Amount of time devoted to community involvement
- Services that are beneficial to individuals and families
- Barriers to accessing support
- Number of individuals who had received mental health and wellness services
- Needs, concerns, and symptoms related to the 12/14 tragedy

The main goal of these questions was to better understand the community's strengths, challenges, and barriers to recovery. A later survey should include the same initial questions, in addition to some relevant to changing perspectives over time. For instance, we asked:

- Do you feel connected to your community?
- Have you participated in community events? Which were helpful?
- What is the most effective way for you to receive information about community events, offerings, and resources?
- What programs have been successful or most helpful to you?
- I am concerned about changes taking place in the community. (Check yes or no.)
- I am receiving mental health and wellness support. (Check yes or no.)
- How beneficial have these services been to you and your family?
- I have some guilt since the tragedy. (Check yes or no.)
- I experience the following symptoms since the tragedy. (Fill in the blank.)
- I could benefit from services but am not receiving them, because I am not ready to reach out. (Check yes or no.)
- My family has benefited from the available funds for services. (Check yes or no.)
- With the knowledge that funding for individual services is time limited, are there concerns that you feel need to be addressed?
- I could use more education about the different groups and organizations that can provide assistance in the community. (Check yes or no.)
- I feel the community is moving forward in a positive way. (Check yes or no.)

The length of your work should dictate how many times you capture and compare findings. Try not to overload your community with more time-consuming surveys than is necessary. Remember that most people are already exhausted, and have added new activities to their daily repertoire since the tragedy. For the most part, people want to get back to their old lives, and hope for a time when they are not reminded of the incident. Also, many people are wary of being asked about recovery and unsure whether taking surveys is value added. When drafting these questionnaires, remember that sometimes less is more: asking a few questions that give you a thorough assessment of your objectives may be more useful than asking many questions that produce too many variables.

When I began to familiarize myself with the community, I heard stories about people who came to town promising assistance they never delivered on, so it helps to identify your purpose in collecting the information and write questions that require simple responses to easily identifiable issues. Obviously you want a high response rate, too, so distributing surveys in a format that is easy to complete, such as email, or snail mail with a self-addressed return envelope, is best.

At the end of our tenure, we wanted to look at our data in an aggregate way. This was beyond my expertise, so we hired a metrics consultant to talk to our board and analyze target measures to provide information about the next phases the town should plan for. We titled the aggregation effort the "Final Metrics Project." The purpose was to examine all the NRRT data to develop business intelligence and analytics regarding the organization's support and outreach services. The project was not a clinical analysis of our services; it was an analysis of data captured by the NRRT in our tracking database and the case notes managed by care coordinators. Specifically, the main objectives were to:

- Define key metrics about NRRT's operations
- Visualize and measure key metrics
- Design a data model that allowed multidimensional analysis of NRRT data
- Complete a trends analysis to forecast key metrics
- Identify any correlations and/or variable relationships
- Provide data collection recommendations for the future, and consider how data could have been better utilized in hindsight

When the final report was released, I was not sure it was as useful as the data analysis generated by our project manager. For instance, the metrics consultant tried to use pieces of data such as repeat visits to our center as a predictor of future need. But we knew many variables are involved in return visits. Repeat visits could indicate that an individual was benefiting positively from a service and following through for a healthy outcome, or that the individual had built up trust in the services and came back to refer a family member.

While this was approved by my board of directors, it was also an example of how they did not fully understand what their role would be moving forward, and how they might be helpful in their extended work. No discussion took place as to whether the board would disband when the Recovery and Resiliency Team completed its grant work, or whether the board would continue to be in place in a new capacity. The metrics project report did allow for a final statistical analysis of who was utilizing services, at what rate, and which specific services were the most requested over time. This had been included in our monthly reports, but was now depicted on an aggregate level over our tenure.

IN SUMMARY

Make data collection a daily practice. Treat it as a priority, but be thoughtful about measuring protocols. Anticipate goals for forecasting present and future needs to the best of your ability. Don't be afraid to build your own program if you cannot find software that captures what you need. And because this is a relatively new field, the data metrics experts may not have all the answers, or may misunderstand statistics you have already graphed.

CHAPTER FOURTEEN

FINAL
THOUGHTS

When the rest of us turned off our televisions to resume normal lives on December 14, 2012, the town of Newtown sat in a haze of devastation. The loss of twenty-six children and adults—all members of the same small community—was unfathomable. Incredibly difficult decisions lay ahead, and shattered lives needed triage. Hundreds were emotionally injured, and the recovery process would take immense support, driven by a dedicated group of professionals who played integral roles in helping the community pick up the pieces and move forward while honoring those who were gone. More than five years later, the wounds in this community are still present, but healing.

There were challenges stepping into this recovery realm eighteen months after the tragedy; a great deal of my energy was devoted to peeling back protective layers the community had built up due to early disappointments and stern conclusions about who to trust, what was value added, and how our team could be most effective to them. We knew from the beginning the NRRT was a temporary resource, though we believe that it should have been ongoing. Research shows that mental health needs for a traumatized community can trace outward as far as ten to fifteen years after an incident occurs. In the twenty months that we existed, we serviced over 900 individuals, and even as our office was closing we had a strong uptick in the number of new clients. Our mandate was to create programs and services that educated the public and remained sustainable after we left. We wanted to create awareness, provide knowledge and resources, and have a lasting impact on the community.

I hope this book is a useful resource for those in a position to care for a community in the wake of a tragedy. It was born out of a belief that sharing my experience engineering the work, along with some of the structure and content of our particular circumstance, can guide other individuals who are called to help a community heal. I am proud of my team's efforts. While our experience can serve as an example for successful programming and procedures, the struggles, challenges, and negative reactions also offer lessons to smooth out the very bumpy road to resiliency. This book was intended to share the basic constructs of building a recovery and resiliency model in the consequence phase of a community tragedy, but I hope it also illustrates the ramifications of complex trauma and complicated grief, and how these concepts informed our response model. My time as the community outreach liaison for the Newtown Recovery and Resiliency Team put me a unique position in the town, where our collective model included a resource bank, individual support, crisis management, community education, large-scale community programs, data collection, staffing, site development, and lots of lessons for recovery about issues such as politics, money, trauma-informed care, vicarious traumatization, the need for ongoing services, and more.

Every community response will be defined by its unique characteristics, including social, economic, and geographic nuances. The concepts I illustrated can be integrated into any recovery response model and tweaked, expanded, or enhanced to best fit other communities. The healing process cannot be adequately addressed without understanding the impact of trauma. And resilience begins only after those consequences are accurately assessed.

When this event occurred, it rocked the nation. The tragedy was so chilling, people thought it would force the country to transcend differences to prevent similar tragedies from occurring in the future. Unfortunately, that did not happen. In the time between the Sandy Hook School shooting and the writing of this book there has been no shortage of additional tragedies, more than 300 of them school shootings. Incredible efforts have been made to bring issues like gun violence prevention, identifying and addressing mental illness concerns, and the impact of trauma exposure to the forefront, and some positive change has occurred. But mass tragedies remain common.

While the hope is that no community encounters a need for this type of healing, we know that such hope is not realistic. Addressing issues based on the lessons we learned, however, can help a community achieve thoughtful, effective, and lasting recovery.

BIBLIOGRAPHY

Lipsky, Laura van Dernoot, and Connie Burk. *Trauma Stewardship: An Everyday Guide to Caring for Self While Caring for Others.* San Francisco: Berrett-Koehler Publishers, 2009

Van der Kolk, Bessel A. *The Body Keeps the Score: Brain, Mind, and Body in the Healing of Trauma.* New York: Viking, 2014

Porges, Stephen W., and Deb A. Dana. *Clinical Applications of the Polyvagal Theory: The Emergence of Polyvagal-informed Therapies.* New York: W. W. Norton & Company, 2018.

Porges, Stephen W. *The Polyvagal Theory: Neurophysiological Foundations of Emotions, Attachment, Communication, and Self-regulation.* New York: W.W. Norton, 2011.

Druck, Ken. *The Real Rules of Life: Balancing Life's Terms with Your Own.* New York: Hay House, 2012.

Ortner, Nick. *The Tapping Solution: A Revolutionary System for Stress-free Living*. New York: Hay House, 2014.

Parkes, Colin Murray. "Elisabeth Kübler-Ross, *On Death and Dying*: A Reappraisal." *Mortality* 18, no. 1 (2013): 94-97. https://doi:10.1080/13576275.2012.758629.

Grand, David. *Brainspotting: The Revolutionary New Therapy for Rapid and Effective Change*. Boulder, CO: Sounds True, 2013.

Gentry, J. Eric. *Forward-Facing Trauma Therapy: Healing the Moral Wound*. Sarasota, FL: Compassion Unlimited, 2016.

"Myptsd.com—My PTSD Forum | A Post Traumatic Stress Disorder (PTSD) Forum Co.." Znwhois.com. Accessed August 31, 2018. https://www.zonwhois.net/www/myptsd.com.html.

Barron, Jill L. "Community Needs Assessment for the Town of Newtown, CT." Accessed August 31, 2018. http://www.newtown-ct.gov/health-department/files/barron-cna-newtown.

"Adverse Childhood Experiences (ACE) Study: Leading Determinants of Health." PsycEXTRA Dataset, 2010. https://doi:10.1037/e604202012-012.

Calhoun, Laurence G., and Richard G. Tedeschi. "Posttraumatic Growth: The Positive Lessons of Loss." In *Meaning Reconstruction & the Experience of Loss*, edited by Robert A. Neimeyer. 157-72. Washington, DC: American Psychological Association, 2001

Silver, Roxane Cohen, E. Alison Holman, Judith Pizarro Andersen, Michael Poulin, Daniel N. McIntosh, and Virginia Gil-Rivas. "Mental- and Physical-Health Effects of Acute Exposure to Media Images of the September 11, 2001, Attacks and the Iraq War." *Psychological Science* 24, no. 9 (2013): 1623-634. https://doi:10.1177/0956797612460406.

CDC Foundation. "CDC 24/7: Saving Lives. Protecting People." Accessed September 01, 2018. https://www.cdcfoundation.org/ cdc-247-saving-lives-protecting-people.